CW01262991

BRIGHT MINDS, BEAUTIFUL IDEAS
Parallel thoughts in different times

ISBN 90 6369 0622

Published by BIS Publishers, Amsterdam

Copyright © 2003 BIS Publishers, Amsterdam
All rights reserved. No part of this publication may be reproduced or
transmitted in any form or by any means, electronic or mechanical, including
photocopy, recording or any information storage and retrieval system,
without permission in writing from the copyright owner(s).

We have tried to exercise all copyrights within the legal requirements.
Nevertheless, anyone who thinks they can claim certain rights can contact us.

Parallel thoughts in different times

BRIGHT MINDS, BEAUTIFUL IDEAS

Bruno Munari, Charles & Ray Eames, Martí Guixé and Jurgen Bey

Edited by Ed Annink
and Ineke Schwartz

EXPERIMENTADESIGN2003
BIENAL DE LISBOA / 17 SET / 02 NOV

Ontwerpwerk
office for design

poi [products of imagination]®

BPI

you can
Canon

Publishing house:
BIS Publishers
Herengracht 370-372
P.O. Box 323
1000 AH Amsterdam
Phone 0031 (20) 524 75 60
Fax 0031 (20) 524 75 57
www.bispublishers.nl
bis@bispublishers.nl

© 2003 BIS Publishers, Amsterdam
ISBN 90 6369 062 2

BISPUBLISHERS

Content

Introduction	7
PARALLEL THOUGHTS IN DIFFERENT TIMES	
Questions and answers, Charles Eames, 1969	12
Questions and answers, Martí Guixé, 2003	14
Questions and answers, Jurgen Bey, 2003	18
Bruno Munari, Fantasy, Invention, Creativity, Imagination, 1977	22
WORKS	
Bruno Munari	27
Timeline 1919-1971	49
Charles & Ray Eames	53
[Personalize this book]	77
Martí Guixé	99
Timeline 1969-2003	167
Jurgen Bey	171
WORKSHOP	218
Martí Guixé and 9 students	223
Jurgen Bey and 9 students	229
Literature	236
Colophon	238
Photocredits	240

Bruno Munari, 1907-1998
Charles & Ray Eames, 1907-1978, 1912-1988
Martí Guixé, 1964
Jurgen Bey, 1965

Introduction
Bright Minds, Beautiful Ideas
Parallel thoughts in different times

Beyond problem solving
The profession of designer is a turbulent one. A designer likes to interact with people (colleagues, airplane captains, bartenders, friends, restaurant keepers, football players, actors, manufacturers, scientists, managers, artists and so on), which together generates many insights and ideas. He or she likes books and magazines and other visual and verbal information of all kinds and from all countries. A designer wants to know what is happening in the world. Who is doing what and above all: why? All his friends are like that. And all perceive the world in different ways, they see differently, interpret differently, explain differently, and decide differently. So, their output is different as well.

Some designers are even beyond problem solving and finding answers for questions asked. They come up with new questions, new viewpoints and new ways to look at things. They bring exciting interpretations about newly-developed materials or new production technologies and, even more, they come up with completely new ways of approaching global and local issues. They are able to develop something that makes an essential contribution to society, that resolves everyday problems or reflects or comments upon them: perhaps in the form of a product, but sometimes a system or guide to tackling familiar things differently.

In this regard, four people currently come to mind – two 'classic' and two 'contemporary' designers: the Italian Bruno Munari (1907-1998), the American couple Charles (1907-1978) & Ray (1912-1988) Eames, the Catalan Martí Guixé (1964) and the Dutchman Jurgen Bey (1965). What they all have in common is the ability to look further than the end of their nose – beyond the world of the drawing table, of commercial operations, marketing and calculations. Besides a shared design standpoint they share a vision of the world, of society and culture, science and economics. They are capable of thinking and working at a global level, not just a local one. They come up with streams of unexpected questions and statements. It is not the diverse branches of industry that make them work. It is their own curiosity that moves them. So doing they move us, their colleagues, their producers and consumers.

Shifts and changes
Such ways of thinking, seeing and doing are of course always important. Because society – and with this culture – is subjected to constant changes, norms and values are continually re-considered and adjusted calling for unconventional visions and approaches. Something that today is needed more than ever. An overcrowded market, shifting disciplines, mixing and merging labels, global economy down and local cultures up are the context of the contemporary designer, consumer and industry. As old ideas are confronted with new practices, even the cultural and economical molochs and stepping stones do not seem to be able to last. Companies are cutting back, firing their workforce, halting innovations and turning their backs on experiment. Over the last few decades, the design industry has produced an enormous amount of products in many materials, colours and qualities. More and more designers entered the design profession and more and more products were made by growing numbers of design enterprises. The mountain of products they made together seems to be a devaluation of design. There are innumerable imitations, epigones and repetitions that nobody seems to need anymore. Almost nothing stands out as a singular exploration, self-willed stance or extraordinary end result. The status of the designer has become nondescript. Designers are not referred to in terms of their originality but in terms of their name and status. Some people don't want to hear the word

'design' and an increasingly number of designers no longer wish to be associated with it.

High time to reconsider the role of the designer and the value and (possible) meanings and values of design. High time for the question of what we really want and need. And not only to serve 'good business' (whatever that may be) because the Western economy is in a slump (only China has undergone economic growth of roughly 6% over recent years) or because of the stifling competition in the market. Even the consumer has simply had enough of the overload. Slowly but surely, the situation is reversing: the initially super-successful mechanism of producing more of the same but-just-that-bit-different, has collapsed. Too much of anything creates inflation: value depreciates, and meaning is lost.

These are difficult points to answer for designers because we want to create. We like to see our ideas distributed globally. Everybody must have our coat hanger! Our car! Our vase! Our chair! But when so many designers more or less have the same handwriting, the same taste, the same talent to create a shape in such a way that it can be produced, and the design industry is confused – what then?

A subjective selection
When Guta Moura Guedes of ExperimentaDesign 2003 invited me, as a member of staff, to devise a project on the theme 'Beyond Consumption' I had an answer at the ready: a project on the mentality and attitude of truly innovative designers. A project that would excite, challenge and inspire another kind of designer mentality. A project about curiosity, investigation, the powers of imagination in combination with the right intuition. A plea for more sensible thinking and less thoughtless production. A challenge to debate the concept 'beautiful', to expand it to include content, meaning and ethics. 'Bright Minds, Beautiful Ideas, parallel thoughts in different times' consists of a workshop, a book, an exhibition and a series of debates. The project centres on the body of thought and work of Bruno Munari, Ray & Charles Eames, Martí Guixé and Jurgen Bey.

Of course this is a personal and therefore highly subjective selection of designers. For which there is good reason. These four are all great examples of vital designers and a vital design mentality, in an artistic and inspiring way as well as in a 'hands on' way that uses the possibilities of science and industry. Designers that don't just talk about taking an inter-disciplinary approach, but who actually succeed in operating within various design disciplines and make work that extends over various social levels.

The work the Eameses has been praised, discussed and published countless times. What we value in the context of this project are not so much the 'leg splint' and the 'DCW chair' that is still a smart addition to any office, but their 'House of Cards' and other children's games; their films, their communication and their interest in science. Plus their ability to undertake things, triggered by their own curiosity, followed by seeking the right arguments to convince the industry to put their proposals into production, not only argued in economic terms, but in cultural and social terms too. With the Eameses, all three were always beautifully balanced. Even if this is not so apparent today, in their days their work was revolutionary although it now predominantly serves as representation.

Munari only incidentally succeeds in combining his passion for culture with commercial production. His mental world, his imaginative powers,

HOW TO EAT PHARMA-SPAMT

ENTER Pharma-Bar · Smell · SALIVA Activates · Breath Continuously · Traga SALIVA · AURA Comes

'Aura'   'Penellessa'

his writings and his machines, however, all hold their value. For example read his great writings in the book *'Bruno Munari, Air Made Visible.'* Munari's work is a substantial source of inspiration for many artists and designers.

Jurgen Bey's greatest quality is his naturally questioning behaviour. By continuously philosophising about what lies beneath familiar things – possibilities, answers, potential and coherence – he raises highly unconventional questions and answers. Sometimes they are usable in designing, sometimes bizarre, but can always be taken equally seriously. Bey is able to table genuinely new insights. His interest in environmental issues, human rules and behaviour do the rest. Martí Guixé is another extremely unconventional thinker. In his self-created vacuum, he can do whatever he wants: magazines, exhibition makers and even the business community are eager to see how he gives shape to the concept 'being really contemporary'. More interested in food and systems than in products, his designs are often immaterial and his interventions minimal. They always embrace far more than the humorous or even corny comments on the world that they're often taken for.

Munari and Eames hit their peaks in the fifties and sixties. Guixé and Bey have only just started. They (still) don't always have an immediately implementable connection to the industry. But they too both have an enormous interest in culture – their insatiable interest in contemporary social developments have a deep social and ethical awareness and an unconventional approach that generates much food for thought. They have ideas with the same energy, decisiveness and humour as Munari and Eames in their day. They merely live in another time that plays by different rules.

CULTURE AND MANDORLA

When Munari created 'Penellessa' he was 53. He looked at the moon and wrote about people's stubborn inflexibility. Why do we see faces in everything and don't see bluebottles in the moon? Because we carry the image of human faces in our immediate consciousness, not images of bluebottles. Munari makes a portrait of a long-bristled brush, the kind you use to create fake wood grain.

By uniting/combining the words 'princess' and 'pencil' he simultaneously creates an appropriate new word that, just like the face, fits precisely into his imaginative world. One thing becomes another – the brush gains character, you see the innocence of the girl hanging there – it's a very moving thing.

Here, Munari is not acting the successful designer. He created an image that perfectly communicates his was of looking and thinking: open, curious, explorative, layered and full of humour. 'Penellessa' is not a product for direct economic use or for instant money flow. It served the purpose of joy, fantasy and imagination. Nor do Munari's so-called *useless machines* 'aid in the creation of capital', as the designer described it himself. 'Some people held that they were extremely useful, in fact, because they produce spiritual consumer goods: images, aesthetic sensibility, education of taste, kinetic information, and so on', he wrote. Martí Guixé has a word for that kind of value: 'Mandorla', or 'aura' in English. To feel good, inspired, touched, fulfilled, content, happy, energetic, are all wonderful offsprings of products, systems and ideas, the economic value of which is often underestimated. In fact the mentality of Martí Guixé touches that of Bruno Munari. They think parallel in different times, as do Ray & Charles Eames and Jurgen Bey. All of them have this great imagination, this ability to invent and to discover.

This book

This is a book about inspiration and ideas and about taking a peek behind the scenes. Because the context in which we operate influences what we talk about, think about and do, it also contains images of encounters, urban landscapes, products, films, exhibitions, etc, etc, photographed by Martí Guixé and Jurgen Bey. We would like to invite you to be the fifth source of inspiration. That is why we included some blank pages for your notes and ideas.

Bumping and bouncing

Some designers have magnificent ideas that reach all the magazines but not the market. They are influential but not economically successful. There are also designers that very successfully reach the international market without being noticed by the magazines. And many in between have all different kinds of talent.

We would like this book to be a challenge to using that talent. Imagine the design world as one of the balls in a billiard game, a little like the image projected by chaos theory. Like any other world it is a big, 3 dimensional, moving and constantly changing puzzle in the shape of a ball. Imagine that ball floating between all the other balls. Where and when do they touch? Can they connect? Is any interaction possible? Most of these ball worlds are at least partly closed to outsiders; it is difficult enough to stay alive on your own ball, is it? So they bump and bounce (who is holding the billiard cue by the way...? – another question) in a space. That space, lets call it 'concept space', is full of ideas and possibilities that form the mass of culture, that keep the balls together. Sometimes the mass thickens and communication slows down, sometimes it runs thin and things go fast. But we might be able to influence that ourselves by reaching out to other balls, other worlds, to meet culture and science and economy and kick-starting an interaction. What we need is solutions to common problems, not simply design for its own sake. For what we need right now in design is a good balance between those three elements, and designers able to shortcut the route in between.

Big kiss for Ineke!

Ed Annink
July 2003

What is design? Questions & Answers

Questions and answers, Charles Eames, 1969
Questions and answers, Martí Guixé, 2003
Questions and answers, Jurgen Bey, 2003

Bruno Munari, Fantasy, Invention, Creativity, Imagination, 1977

What is design? Questions & Answers
Madame Amic – Charles Eames 1969

From the book *'Eames Design, the work of the office of Charles and Ray Eames'*. Page 14 and 15.

The following questions were asked by Madame Amic and answered by Charles Eames. The questions and answers were the conceptual basis for the exhibition 'What is design?' in 1969 at the Musée des Arts Décoratifs.

Q1 What is your definition of 'Design'?
A A plan for arranging elements in such a way as to best accomplish a particular purpose.

Q2 Is design an expression of art (an art form)?
A The design is an expression of the purpose. It may (if it is good enough) later be judged as art.

Q3 Is design a craft for industrial purposes?
A No – but design may be a solution to some industrial problems.

Q4 What are the boundaries of design?
A What are the boundaries of problems?

Q5 Is design a discipline that concerns itself with only one part of the environment?
A No.

Q6 Is it a method of general expression?
A No – it is a method of action.

Q7 Is design a creation of an individual?
A No – because to be realistic one must always admit the influence of those who have gone before.

Q8 … or creation of a group?
A Often.

Q9 Is there design ethic?
A There are always design constraints and these usually include an ethic.

Q10 Does design imply the idea of products that are necessarily useful?
A Yes – even though the use might be very subtle.

Q11 Is it able to cooperate in the creation of works reserved solely for pleasure?
A Who would say that pleasure is not useful?

Q12 Ought from to derive from the analysis of function?
A The great risk here is that the analysis may not be complete.

Q13 Can the computer substitute for the designer?
A Probably, in some special cases, but usually the computer is an aid to the designer.

Q14 Does design imply industrial manufacture?
A Some designs do and some do not- depending on the nature of the design and the requirements.

Q15 Is design an element of industrial policy?
A Certainly; as is any other aspect of quality, obvious or subtle, of the product. It seems that anything can be an element in policy.

Q16 Ought design to care about lowering costs?
A A product often becomes more useful if the costs are lowered without harming quality.

Q17 Does the creation of design admit constraint?
A Design depends largely on constraints.

Q18 What constraints?
A The sum of all constraints. Here is one of the few effective keys to the design problem – the ability of the designer to recognize as many of the constraints as possible – his willingness and enthusiasm for working within these constraints – the constraint of price, of size, of strength, balance, of surface, of time, etc; each problem has it own peculiar list.

Q19 Does design obey laws?
A Aren't constraints enough?

Q20 Are there tendencies and schools in design?
A Yes, but this is more a human frailty than an ideal.

Q21 Ought the final product to bear the trademark of the designer? of the research office?
A In some cases, one may seem appropriate. In some cases, the other, and certainly in some cases, both.

Q22 What is the relation of design to the world of fashion (current trends)?
A The objects of fashion have usually been designed with the particular constraint of fashion in mind.

Q23 Is design ephemeral?
A Some needs are ephemeral. Most designs are ephemeral.

Q24 Ought it to tend towards the ephemeral or towards permanence?
A Those needs and designs that have a more universal quality will tend toward permanence.

Q25 To whom does design address itself: to the greatest number (the masses)? to the specialists or the enlightened amateur? to a privileged social class?
A To the need.

Q26 Can public action aid the advancement of design?
A The proper public action can advance most anything.

Q27 After having answered all these questions, do you feel you have been able to practice the profession of 'design' under satisfactory conditions, or even optimum conditions?
A Yes.

Q28 Have you been forced to accept compromises?
A I have never been forced to accept compromises but I have willingly accepted constraints.

Q29 What do you feel is the primary condition for the practice of design and it's propagation?
A Recognition of need.

Q30 What is the future of design?
A [no answer]

What is design? Questions & Answers
Ineke Schwartz – Martí Guixé 2003

The 30 questions about design, the approach to design and the design process, that were answered in 1969 by Charles Eames, are now put to Martí Guixé. The questions have been reformulated here and there to bring them more in line with the issues currently confronting design.

Q1 In 1969 Charles Eames was asked: What is your definition of 'Design'?
Today I want to ask you: What is your definition of design?
A For me design is a kind of submission you make to the economy when doing projects. As an ex-designer I am free from that, I don't need to follow this parameter. But I very much like playing with it, to make that economy submit to me.

Q2 In 1969 Charles Eames was asked: Is design an expression of art (an art form)?
Today I want to ask you: Is design an expression of economy?
A Yes. A product – which is anything you can sell or negotiate, not just objects – is always in a context that you consume.

Q3 In 1969 Charles Eames was asked: Is design a craft for industrial purposes?
Today I want to ask you: Is design capable to change a company's opinion?
A Yes. As long as you, designer, make sure that the company makes some form of economic profit, they accept anything.

Q4 In 1969 Charles Eames was asked: What are the boundaries of design?
Today I want to ask you: What are the boundaries of design?
A Any ware can be designed. As in our contemporary world everything is ware – lifestyle, feelings and opinion are concepts you can buy – everything can be designed.

Q5 In 1969 Charles Eames was asked: Is design a discipline that concerns itself with only one part of the environment?
Today I want to ask you: Should design be influenced by the phenomenon of buying and possessing?
A If you do something that is not for production, you are not designing. Buying is OK, but possessing is about representation, and I think for an individual this is related only to the body, and no longer connected to static non-personal objects. But companies, they need representation.

Q6 In 1969 Charles Eames was asked: Is it a method of general expression?
Today I want to ask you: Is design something that relates to consumers' individual expression?
A If it makes the consumption more successful, yes.

Q7 In 1969 Charles Eames was asked: Is design a creation of an individual?
Today I want to ask you: How original can a designer be?
A Very. It depends how complex you are and if you design aura or a very functional product like a toothbrush. Though also that could be completely original, for nowadays everything is boring, commercial and conventional.

Q8 In 1969 Charles Eames was asked: ...or creation of a group?
Today I skip this question: Do you need a question in order to design?
A You need a question, but of course you can make your own. Usually design is a problem-solving discipline and Art a trouble-making one. In both you are confronted with a situation where you react, solving or sabotaging. But you can solve sabotaging, and sabotage by solving.

Q9 In 1969 Charles Eames was asked: Is there design ethic?
Today I want to ask you: What is your design ethic?
A   Be contemporary.

Q10 In 1969 Charles Eames was asked: Does design imply the idea of products that are necessarily useful?
Today I want to ask you: Does design have to be beautiful?
A   What is beautiful to you? This is a neo-colonialist question. Are you trying to tell me what should be beautiful to me? Colonization through aesthetics is a consequence of globalisation. Also for this reason I work more with systems, which are open and formless.

Q11 In 1969 Charles Eames was asked: Is it able to cooperate in the creation of works reserved solely for pleasure?
Today I want to ask you: Can the process of design be for pure pleasure?
A   Yes.

Q12 In 1969 Charles Eames was asked: Ought form to derive from the analysis of function?
Today I want to ask you: Do we need less from as we need more from less?
A   Depending on what.

Q13 In 1969 Charles Eames was asked: Can the computer substitute for the designer?
Today I want to ask you: How much computer do you need?
A   I need a computer for communicating globally. But everything is communication.

Q14 In 1969 Charles Eames was asked: Does design imply industrial manufacture?
Today I want to ask you: Does design mean industrial manufacture?
A   Yes – if not, it is craftsmanship or art.

Q15 In 1969 Charles Eames was asked: Is design an element of industrial policy?
Today I want to ask you: Is design able to change the perceptions of society?
A   Generally not. Generally design is only a banal tool; if it changes the world it is not design. Art or politics can change society – and an ex-designer.

Q16 In 1969 Charles Eames was asked: Ought design to care about lowering costs?
Today I want to ask you: Should design be affordable?
A   Yes, but what happens in the last years is that design is only associated with luxurious items, and well-designed cheap products don't have a distribution network. There is no opportunity of buying good, well-designed, cheap products in a standard supermarket. Economy doesn't understand good design.

Q17 In 1969 Charles Eames was asked: Does the creation of design admit constraint?
Today I want to ask you: Does society in itself place limitations on design?
A   There are a lot of taboos still to break.

Q18 In 1969 Charles Eames was asked: What constraints?
Today I want to ask you: What are your design limitations?
A   No limits.

Q19 In 1969 Charles Eames was asked: Does design obey laws?
Today I want to ask you: Which design laws are left?
A   That depends on what kind of designer you are. In my world I make and break my own laws.

Q20   In 1969 Charles Eames was asked: Are there tendencies and schools in design?
Today I want to ask you: Can tendencies (streams) in design add new values in society?
A   Tendencies are just stupid values created by empty trend magazines, which they just copy. They can only turn society more stupid.

Q21   In 1969 Charles Eames was asked: Ought the final product to bear the trademark of the designer? Of the research office?
Today I want to ask you: How much of Narcissus has to survive in you?
A   Brands are part of the game.

Q22   In 1969 Charles Eames was asked: What is the relation of design to the world of fashion (current trends)?
Today I want to ask you: Does design need its own time rhythm?
A   Rhythms belong to economy. It depends if you are designing a shoe or a theme park.

Q23   In 1969 Charles Eames was asked: Is design ephemeral?
Today I want to ask you: Is design in?
A   Only among designers.

Q24   In 1969 Charles Eames was asked: Ought it to tend towards the ephemeral or towards permanence?
Today I want to ask you: What should be the real durability of design?
A   The durability of the material that the product is made of. If there is no material it can re-adapt more easily.

Q25   In 1969 Charles Eames was asked: To whom does design address itself: to the greatest number (the masses)? to the specialists or the enlightened amateur? to a privileged social class?
Today I want to ask you: Is design a global or a local phenomenon?
A   It is a banal and hyper real phenomenon. It is banal because it helps you to make your ultra-local life more comfortable and decadent – for example the one that occurs in your kitchen. And it is hyper real because using the media it builds an illusion of reality that tries to tell you what your life should look like.

Q26   In 1969 Charles Eames was asked: Can public action aid the advancement of design?
Today I want to ask you: Is awareness of society a tool in design?
A   Awareness is a tool only in neo-liberal ideology or in the 3rd world. Design is not only for designing tools.

Q27   In 1969 Charles Eames was asked: After having answered all these questions, do you feel you have been able to practice the profession of 'design' under satisfactory conditions, or even optimum conditions?
Today I want to ask you: Do you have anything you would like to add to the design world?
A   As an ex-designer I am not interested in the design world. I do my project and I don't care about what other designers do. I am also not a design consumer, so I am not updated about what is going on. I like to consume, though, like restaurants and bars.

Q28   In 1969 Charles Eames was asked: Have you been forced to accept compromises?
Today I want to ask you: What compromises do you accept?
A   Everything is a compromise. I do not accept them, I deal with them.

Q29 In 1969 Charles Eames was asked: What do you feel is the primary condition for the practice of design and its propagation?
Today I want to ask you: Can a designer be an intermediary between economy and culture today?

A Economy needs culture, because nobody intelligent believes in economy anymore. That's why a designer should deal with culture today, but there is no meeting point between economy and culture. What happens is just the mercantilization of culture for economy. In the end the designer is the murderer of culture.

Q30 In 1969 Charles Eames was asked: What is the future of design?
Today I want to ask you: Is there a meaning in creating?

A To survive convention!

What is design? Questions & Answers
Ineke Schwartz – Jurgen Bey 2003

For the 1969 design exhibition 'What is Design' Charles Eames was asked the following questions, in order to gain a greater understanding of his approach to the design process. These questions have been re-formulated for contemporary design practice.

Q1 In 1969 Charles Eames was asked: What is your definition of 'Design'? Today I want to ask you: What is your definition of design?
A Design means to give shape to the manmade world.

Q2 In 1969 Charles Eames was asked: Is design an expression of art (or an art form)? Today I want to ask you: Is design an expression of economics?
A Design is born of economics. I hope the time has come to begin to develop a more social aspect.

Q3 In 1969 Charles Eames was asked: Is design a craft for industrial purposes? Today I want to ask you: Is design capable of changing a company's outlook?
A It is when the designer takes a clear point of view. As a designer you should critically rephrase the questions posed to you by the company and by so doing you can change the company's outlook.

Q4 In 1969 Charles Eames was asked: What are the boundaries of design? Today I want to ask you: What are the boundaries of design?
A There are no boundaries except the minds of the designer and his client.

Q5 In 1969 Charles Eames was asked: Is design a discipline that concerns itself with only one part of the environment? Today I want to ask you: Should design be influenced by the phenomenon of acquisition and ownership?
A No, but the designer should be aware of the seduction of the acquisition and ownership phenomenon and have an opinion on this.

Q6 In 1969 Charles Eames was asked: Is design a method of general expression? Today I want to ask you: Is design something that relates to the consumers' individual expression?
A Everything people buy is a personal choice and therefore a form of self-expression. The difference with contemporary design is that there is an enormous entourage of marketing and lifestyle magazines attached to it.

Q7 In 1969 Charles Eames was asked: Is design a creation of an individual? Today I want to ask you: How original can a designer be?
A A designer can never be original. Everything I use or apply comes from the existing world; I simply give it a personal touch but I don't invent anything. A designer's greatest achievement is to change the perspective of things a little.

Q8 In 1969 Charles Eames was asked: ...or is design the creation of a group? Today I skip this question. I have another one: Do you need a question in order to design?
A Yes, without questions there are no answers, so you need loads of questions. Of course you can ask them yourself and many are created through circumstances and life itself.

Q9 In 1969 Charles Eames was asked: Is there design ethic? Today I want to ask you: What is your design ethic?
A I believe in the world and in humanity and that is why I make things for people. But always for a specific part of the world. I don't believe in something for everybody:

these are grey things that no one is enthusiastic about and no one likes. I look for what I think is needed. If people don't like it they should stay away or say something during the design process stage. Otherwise it is a waste of time and energy. Employers also share the responsibility here.

Q10   In 1969 Charles Eames was asked: Does design imply the idea of products that are necessarily useful?
Today I want to ask you: Does design have to be beautiful?

A   Yes but the question is what is beauty? In some cases things have to be very ugly, for example, when you want to keep people away from a particular place.

Q11   In 1969 Charles Eames was asked: Is design able to co-operate in the creation of works reserved solely for pleasure?
Today I want to ask you: Can the process of design be for pure pleasure?

A   The design process itself can be purely for pleasure, but the object designed is not, it has other purposes. It cannot become how the advertising world now sees it: everything that's sold must be funny, nothing seems to take itself seriously anymore and there's no explanation of what something can or cannot do – it's dreadful!

Q12   In 1969 Charles Eames was asked: Ought form to derive from the analysis of function?
Today I want to ask you: Do we need less from more, as we need more from less?

A   Nonsense, at a party for example, you want al kinds of stupid stuff around you.
It depends on all kinds of factors.

Q13   In 1969 Charles Eames was asked: Can the computer substitute for the designer?
Today I want to ask you: How much do you need the computer?

A   Quite a lot: I use the computer to organise the business, as a presentation tool, a way of sketching and as a communication tool.

Q14   In 1969 Charles Eames was asked: Does design imply industrial manufacture?
Today I want to ask you: Does design mean industrial manufacture?

A   No, design means: for sale.

Q15   In 1969 Charles Eames was asked: Is design an element of industrial policy?
Today I want to ask you: Is design able to change the perception of society?

A   You should always start with something you want to change. Changing society's perception should be part of your goal when you have to solve problems or if you want to create beauty.

Q16   In 1969 Charles Eames was asked: Ought design to care about lowering costs?
Today I want to ask you: Should design be affordable?

A   What is affordable? Not everything needs to be bought by everyone. We always need things to aspire to.

Q17   In 1969 Charles Eames was asked: Does the creation of design admit constraint?
Today I want to ask you: Does society pose limitations on design?

A   I haven't found them yet.

Q18   In 1969 Charles Eames was asked: What constraints?
Today I want to ask you: What are your design limitations?

A   These are my personal limitations - doubt or the fear of making mistakes.

Q19   In 1969 Charles Eames was asked: Does design obey laws?
Today I want to ask you: Are there any design laws left?

A   No idea, I believe in the language of things; these are my laws. As a designer you have to know how people behave, how they react, and what products they want. If you observe these things, you can understand them: they speak a language that describes what they can do, what they want, where they come from and why they are here. If you study the language, you can get to know them and value them without judging them to be beautiful or ugly.

Q20 In 1969 Charles Eames was asked: Are there tendencies and schools in design?
Today I want to ask you: Can tendencies (streams) in design add new values in society?
A   Yes, a while ago design became influential and this led to the recognition of the value of the concept and now ideas like beauty and ornament are taken seriously again.

Q21 In 1969 Charles Eames was asked: Ought the final product to bear the trademark of the designer, or of the research office?
Today I want to ask you: How much of Narcissus has survived in you?
A   I need a reason to exist, so Narcissus is part of me.

Q22 In 1969 Charles Eames was asked: What is the relation of design to the world of fashion (current trends)?
Today I want to ask you: Does design need its own time rhythm?
A   Some designers and disciplines have their own rhythms, others don't. I have great admiration for artists, who continue stubbornly to do their own thing regardless; who believe in something and want to communicate it.

Q23 In 1969 Charles Eames was asked: Is design ephemeral? Today I want to ask you: Is design 'in'?
A   Yes, we are bombarded by it. Everyone has an opinion about it and we are overwhelmed by it through magazines and television.

Q24 In 1969 Charles Eames was asked: Ought design tend towards the ephemeral or towards permanence?
Today I want to ask you: What is the real durability of design?
A   It should last for as long as it is in use.

Q25 In 1969 Charles Eames was asked: To whom does design address itself: to the greatest number (the masses), to the specialists, the enlightened amateur or to a privileged social class?
Today I want to ask you: Is design a global or a local phenomenon?
A   It is very global but it is time for it to become local. Global phenomena are always the same everywhere. Local concerns itself with the possibilities of the Galapagos Islands for example, where special things can develop undisturbed.

Q26 In 1969 Charles Eames was asked: Can public action aid the advancement of design?
Today I want to ask you: Is awareness of society a tool for design?
A   Without a context things will not function [nothing functions in isolation, if something is not in the right place people will not understand its purpose]. Design is meant for people, so awareness of society is a must.

Q27 In 1969 Charles Eames was asked: After having answered all these questions, do you feel you have been able to practice the profession of 'design' under satisfactory conditions, or even optimum conditions?
Today I want to ask you: Do you have anything you would like to add to the design world?
A   One day I would like to design something that ought to have been created already.

Q28 In 1969 Charles Eames was asked: Have you been forced to accept compromises?
Today I want to ask you: What compromises do you accept?
A Only my own limitations.

Q29 In 1969 Charles Eames was asked: What do you feel is the primary condition for the practice of design and its propagation?
Today I want to ask you: Can a designer today be an intermediary between economy and culture?
A Yes.

Q30 In 1969 Charles Eames was asked: What is the future of design?
Today I want to ask you: Is there a meaning in creating?
A We can not live without change and creating. Society will always have new questions and a demand for answers for which we breed creative minds and bodies.

Bruno Munari
Fantasy, Invention, Creativity, Imagination

Fantasy is the freest of the faculties; in fact, it doesn't even have to concern itself with what it has thought up. It's free to think anything, even the most absurd, incredible, or impossible things. Invention uses the same technique as fantasy – that is, the relation between the things one knows – but it aims it toward a practical use. You invent a new motor, a chemical formula, a material, an instrument, and so on. The inventor, however, doesn't worry about the aesthetic side of his invention. What's important to him is that the invention should actually function and serve some purpose. Sometimes even the inventor concerns himself with the aesthetic side, but, like the famous steam machine in neoclassical style, in the Museo della Scienza e della Technica in Milan, it displays a useless preoccupation with aesthetics, and, above all, merges art and technology in a way that's thought to be mistaken today. In other cases the product of the invention is 'decorated' by an artist, as in the case of the first sewing machine of the art nouveau period that had decoration applied in gold and mother-of-pearl. Perhaps something should also be said about invention and discovery. To invent means to think of something that didn't exist before. To discover means to find something that one didn't know about before, but which already existed. One can say, for example, that Galileo invented telescope with which he discovered that Jupiter has satellites.

Creativity is also an end use of fantasy – indeed of fantasy and of invention – in a global way. Creativity is used in the field of design, considering design as a means of planning, a means that, being free like fantasy and exact like invention, includes all aspects of a problem, not only image as fantasy, not only function as invention, but also the psychological, social, economic, and human aspects. One can speak of design as the projection of an object, a symbol, an environment, a new didactics, a planning method for resolving collective needs, and so on.
[...]

Imagination is the means of visualizing, of rendering visible what fantasy, invention, and creativity devise. In certain individuals imagination is very tenuous, in others fervid and alert, while in others it goes beyond thought. Some people are so devoid of imagination that professionals exist to visualize for them what fantasy, creativity, or invention have dreamed up. in all publicity agencies there are visualizers – designers whose function it is to prepare the sketches or models to show clients so that they, too, can, visualize the end result. There are also modelers who construct full-size or scale models of objects or large constructions, like a bridge or a house, that have been created by the designer. Thus, even these unimaginative people can see a designer's idea, the fruit of fantasy, invention, or creativity. The means of substitution available to the imagination are therefore drawing, painting, sculpture, modeling, film, kinetic art, and so on.

While fantasy, invention, and creativity produce something that didn't exist before, imagination can also imagine something that already exists but that at the moment is not with us; imagination isn't necessarily creative. There are even cases in which the imagination fails to visualize a fantastic thought. Let's take an example: let's try to imagine a wooden motorcycle: the imagination can do this. You could also imagine a glass motorcycle, a completely transparent motorcycle (like those models of the human body in which you can see all the organs). But if you pass from solid material to liquid material and think of a liquid motorcycle… you can't visualize this, no matter how hard the imagination tries. Think of how many people see a face in the moon. Why only a face? Why not a peacock? A dung beetle? Because the dung beetle is never seen, it's not present in people's minds and therefore it's not recognized, while the human face is the first thing that a person sees on seeing the world. It's the first image that's committed to memory, that everyone memorizes, and therefore to say that you see a face in the moon is among the simplest connections that you can make. What do

we see in the stains on walls, in the fragments of
marble that make up certain pavements, in certain
rocks, in certain clouds? Often a face. Someone
sees a whale that is transformed into a camel.

Bruno Munari, Fantasia (1977)

Ineke Schwartz - Martí Guixé, Lisbon, Portugal, May 21th 2003

Ineke Schwartz - Jurg   03

Bruno Munari

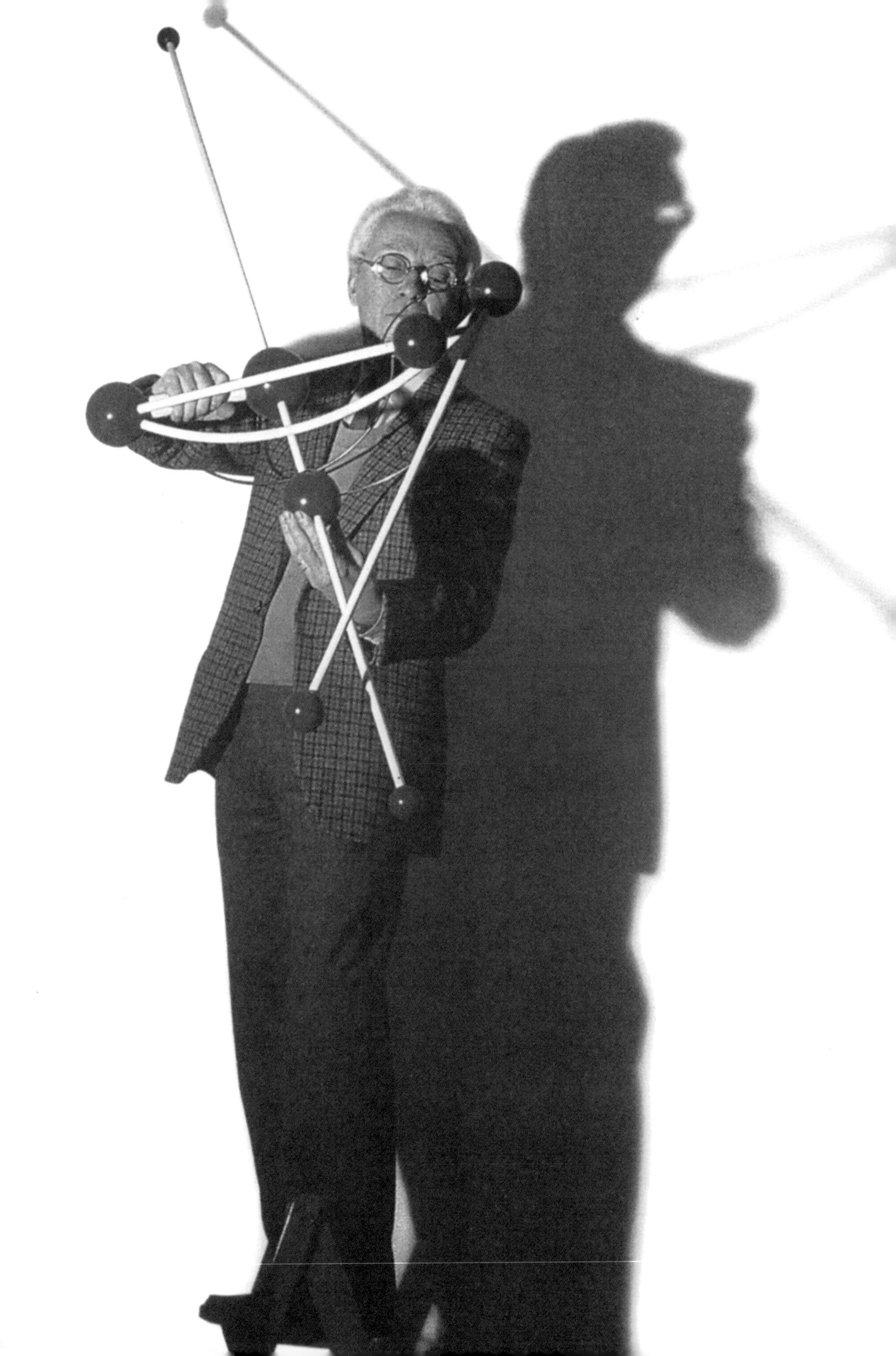

Bruno Munari

Bruno Munari: Design as art?
Munari is certainly not a name that immediately springs to the public mind when it comes to important designers. But ask any world famous designer who was an important source of inspiration that helped form his intellectual character, and there's a good chance he will mention his name. The Italian artist, writer, designer, architect, graphic designer, educator and philosopher Bruno Munari (1907-1998) had, and still has, a great influence on the world of design as we know it today.

As a designer, Munari has a varied array of work to his name – everything from children's toys to lamps, magazines and books. But it isn't his products that are considered his chief contribution to the design world. In all things, Munari was an inspirational thinker and the first critic to see design as a coherent whole of demand, process and thinking, with which it became totally separate from the product. And that in a time in which designers were only rewarded if they came up with beautiful, commercially successful objects. With this, Munari laid the foundation for a design discipline that could be mobilised across a broad social scala (an approach which has since be argued by many) and for a multi-faceted, unconventional approach. Starting out as an artist who also designed, Munari ultimately opted for design. With this he was an interdisciplinary designer avant la lettre. For him, it was very natural to think across different disciplines and combine them. He also studied philosophy and pedagogy, a fascination resulting in scores of children's books, among other things. For designers who question over-consumption and the 'glossy' role currently assigned to designers, Munari's fascination with the design process, for 'obvious' products and his lack of interest in aestheticising end products is an inspiration. For artists, his ideas on the isolation of avant garde art and how to break out of it are an important source. Moreover the way in which Munari proposed integrating craftsmanship and traditions in a contemporary way of thinking without a shred or nostalgia is still always a highly usable starting point. Munari's entirely personal way of approaching the discipline seems more than ever to serve as an attractive example to designers to continue questioning and developing different slants on familiar things.

In the twenties and thirties, his formative years, Munari was both a renowned Italian artist and a designers' designer: reputed among the experts but still not well known to the public at large. Sucked into the dynamic creativity of the activist artists' group the Futurists, he was familiar with the emergence of modern art in Italy and especially with the world of galleries, exhibitions, publications and lectures that made the functioning of art possible. His contact with the Futurists brought him into contact with the *agit-prop* methods with which they confronted and awakened the (often unsuspecting) public. Munari learned that people respond to jokes and modest provocations and that a large section of the public held views on the new culture of the avant garde.

After the Second World War, when modern art became successful and thereby institutionalised, he became disenchanted with the possibilities of what had initially seemed a promising artistic experiment which he felt was gradually conforming to the new rules and forms of expression of the avant garde. In the end, he abandoned the profession of artist, and with it his own artistic practice. By dubbing the designer rather than the artist the artistic pioneer of the new era, he went dramatically far. 'The designer is […] the artist of today', wrote Munari in *'Design as Art,'* the now world-famous book of short texts that he wrote for the newspaper *Il Giorno* wrote. 'Not because he is a genius but because he works in such a way as to re-establish contact between art and the public, because he has the humility and ability to respond to whatever demand is made of him by the society in which he lives, because he knows his job, and the ways and means of solving each problem of design. And finally because he responds to the human needs of his time, and helps people to solve certain problems without stylistic preconceptions or false notions of artistic dignity derived from the schism of arts.'

The Artist and the Etruscan Vase

Going entirely against the trend, in the fifties, Munari thus argued for the abolition of the artist as visionary genius and he crowned the designer of ordinary products as the medium of contemporary culture par excellence. This was quite an accomplishment in the time of Picasso, Miro and Dali who were positioned as geniuses and often behaved accordingly. Munari saw that differently; a new time called for a new type of applied artist. 'Culture today is becoming a mass affair, and the artist must step down from his pedestal and be prepared to make a sign for a butcher's shop (if he knows how to do it)', said Munari in *'Design as Art.'* He made considerable work of stripping the concept of the artist and his role, in both a classic and modern sense, of its mystical connotations. Apart from a hazy term like 'spirit of the age' he turned to history for evidence. As his admirer Umberto Eco many years later demystified the murals of Pompeii as nothing more than adverts for carpentry workshops and brothels, so Munari offered the example of the Etruscan vase that had earned a place in our display cases with its refined form and decoration, but which in the years after it's creation was simply used to store oil. This *schism of art* was, according to Munari, the cause of the fact that art had lost its purpose, its social impact and had alienated the public – in short, a new *l'art pour l'art* had arisen. Precisely the complaints with which today's artists are still struggling. Munari was well ahead of his time. The artist had to become a designer but without importing his artistic codes and methods into his new 'field of investigation and curiosity'. The rules, conditions and methods of designers were less sacred to him. Industrial designers in particular and emphatically craft-minded practitioners of arts and crafts were especially targeted.

Munari made a detailed analysis of the current relations in the worlds of art and design and collapsed the myths that went with them. He lucidly underlined that, in France, the profession of industrial designer had never become free from the traditional applied arts and were thus still closely linked with the fine arts. The real industrial designers in France were anonymous but what was presented at exhibitions was showy artistry with a forced craftsmanship. In France, people designed lamps in arty abstract shapes, sneered Munari, taking no account of the fact that a lamp is meant to give light. Others created surrealist televisions, Dada tables and 'informal' articles of furniture, reflecting the tendencies in modern art but neglecting to give each object its own, specific function. The fact that the design profession in France was called 'Esthetique Industrielle' spoke volumes, felt Munari.

Munari's loathing of this pseudo artistic attitude of artist-designers was eclipsed by his disgust of designers who accepted the commercial fashionability of products with what was almost lethargy. Munari felt that objects should be ordinary and not unnecessarily prettified. Commercial designers – *stylists* in the jargon of the sixties, often of American origin – were guilty of this. According to Munari, they let themselves be entirely swallowed up by the cycle of the economy and used the same trick over and over. 'What most interests a stylist is line, sculptural form, a bizarre idea. A little science fiction does no harm and a sense of elegance is basic'. In just a few words, Munari typified the working methods of stylists in his article *Pure and Applied* published in the sixties, with which he primarily challenged the commercial complacency of these designers. Where he applauded every attempt of artists to escape the typical economic carousel 'Artist – Dealer – Critic – Gallery – Collector', he reproached the designer who was not sufficiently aware of the impact of the urgent rhythm of the fashionable product.

Fashionable and modern society

Munari was one of the first intellectuals in the cultural arena to voice downright criticism of the consumer society's complacent 'progress-mindedness'. The phenomenon of trend was ultimately Munari's most important topic. His rejection of new for the sake of new, the constant production of variants on a theme was an open secret. "What does fashion actually do?", he rhetorically asks in *'Design as Art,'* "It sells you a suit made of material that could last five years, and as soon you have bought it, it tells you that you can't wear it any longer because a newer one has already been created. The same principle can be used to sell anything." This rejection of fads and fancies was shared by others, but Munari was one of the few to devise possible solutions. Like Charles and Ray Eames and his fellow countrymen Gio Ponti and Ettore Sottsass, Munari was convinced of people's ability to distinguish. 'Real', 'original' products would be recognised and valued and their consumers would feel freed by them. If only sufficient products were created that were a 'purpose fit' in a cultural and objective sense, the trendy side of commerce and the disfiguration of the pseudo artistry would be unmasked. Obsessed with the idea of making a positive contribution to society as an artist and designer, his hands itched to put these thoughts into practice.

Munari deliberately first chose the American, then the French practice, to illustrate what he loathed. Design and products could, for him, not be seen separate to the social context in which they arose. Munari used Japan as an example of the opposite of the modern consumer society. In Japan he recognised a modern society that, according to Munari, was in full harmony with the products it used and where designers played a respected role. In that process, closely interwoven with social structure and social development, the Western idea of progress didn't actually exist. In Japan, there was still considerable awe of the craftsmanship of the old masters, one of the reasons for the famous Japanese urge to emulate – even today – while in the West, in the sixties and fifties, experience let alone repetition, had begun to be suspect. Originality and innovation were synonymous with improvement.

Munari's understanding of the word 'new' was different. For him: progress means simplifying not complicating.
The slow and gradual development of products and society lacked, he felt, the fashionable aspects of the new, which he considered positive. This is why he argued for products that naturally related to daily life in contrast to products that were to win a place in the public's hearts by virtue of appearance or marketing – which most designers of the time condoned, and still do.

An everyday utopia

A designer fully integrated into society, who was anonymous and equal to the producer and buyer – this was the ideal Munari held up to his colleagues. Products and design methods had to relate to social developments and not be style-dependent. "A designer with a personal style, arrived at *a priori*, is a contradiction in terms", he declared firmly in *'Design as Art.'* "There is no such thing as a personal style in a designer's work. While a job is in hand, be it a lamp, a radio set, an electric gadget or an experimental object, his sole concern is to arrive at the solution suggested by the thing itself and its destined use. Therefore different things will have different forms, and these will be determined by their different uses and the different materials and techniques employed." This sounds like the method of a problem-solving designer who, on the basis of analyses, attempts to design a sufficiently functioning product. But this isn't what Munari meant. He, like no one else, understood that with his demands of the modern designer he had in fact created an impossible situation. The anonymous designer who made products and improved them, passing them on from father to son, existed by the grace of the innocence and ignorance of his own position. His attitude is "that's how my father worked and that's how

I work". A conscious striving for the conditions that enabled the anonymous designer to exist – the status of ignorance and naturalness – can never be consciously realised.

Designers like Achile Castiglioni and Vico Magistretti, who did their best to design such anonymous, non-designed products, were aiming for the impossible. Their peasant chair, trestle table or bottle opener were almost original but not entirely, like actors using the Stanislavski method to 'become' a fishmonger, taxi driver or street whore. Wonderful products maybe have resulted, but originated from the studios of famous designers, and sold with a designer label. Stylised products that Munari pulled to pieces: "It is probably the desire to get back into society, to re-establish contact with their neighbours, to create an art for everyone and not just for the chosen few with bags of money." It was a strange situation. Famous designers wanted to create anonymous products that were absurdly expensive. They showed just how impossible the new direction was.

For societies where the relationship between maker and user was still very direct and, in contrast to Europe and the US, unbroken, Munari had an almost jealous admiration. But the products that belonged to such a utopic situation could, he believed, still be found all over the world. For a long time, he sought for, and created, a wonderful world-famous collection of locks, coffee machines, fishing nets, forks, spoons, knives, bottles and furniture, each object whose function and use was instantly recognisable even if their makers and origin was unknown. They were not strictly connected to any one culture, unfashionable and probably timeless.
The collection travelled the world and became a renowned ambassador for the ideal of the anonymous designer. Munari's finest hour arrived when he managed to convince the jurors of the prestigious Italian design prize, the 'Compasso d'Oro' (regularly awarded to an illustrious designer) to give that year's prize to 'the anonymous designer'.

For the first time there was no new big name, no overly familiar commercial or 'well' designed product but recognition of insight and of an unachievable result.

The sea and the child
Even though consciously unconscious design was impossible, Munari saw other opportunities for being an 'unspoilt' designer. Simplicity and understandability were important – users shouldn't be fatigued by complex ideas on products and intentions, found Munari. Those were concepts for which designers of all kinds argued for at the time, but the simplicity of Munari had little to do with the often apparently simple form that most others worked towards. He was concerned with ease of action, user-friendliness, lucidity and consistency of thought. Munari proposed that users and designers should follow simple ways of thinking that, if they were logically used, would lead to working results that would often literally appeal to the imagination. 'Logical' here means Munari logic – logic with a specific natural and human self-evidence. The notion of his *Useless Machine* was based on reversing the thought that an ordinary machine is intended to generate money or at least make boring work easier. Munari made a machine with all the attractions of a machine but that produced nothing and with this entered into a debate on technological progress and its practical expressions, without being pedantic.

Every question and every assignment requires a systematic approach, asserts Munari, with which he meant that every issue has its own logic. To make this way of working more understandable, he often referred to the methods of children and nature, generally understandable, eloquent illustrations that in his hands often produced surprising results.

For Munari, 'child' and 'nature' are key concepts that are models for two equally important but different ways of thinking that could serve as a starting point. In nature, it was the naturalness with which life develops; Munari recognised in this a way of designing of which the speed – or rather the total lack of it – fascinated him. For Munari nature has various manifestations but never that of divine nature to which so many designers turn to legitimise certain formal proportions.

For Munari the method of the child represented a way of approaching the world. Like a child, he met everything with curiosity and surprise. He questioned everything, went on questioning and assumed new and unusual standpoints. This is a totally different standing point than that of the designer who works from the perspective of knowledge and insights. Munari designed based on the first confrontation with his subject. He presented the results not as complete products but as parts of a mental world where the viewer or user often understood his questions and approach immediately.

That the results of these two starting points were so fresh was mainly due to the fact that Munari was capable of formulating interesting questions then following a clear, understandable and consistent design path. For instance, Munari designed books that were dubbed 'unreadable' but that are only so in comparison with readable books. The expectation of readability in the form of words and pictures is crushed on page one: these are charming, elegant and unusual books about the structure, lay-out and visualisation and discussion of how books are put together.

The idea of useless machines originates in the surprising and totally logical consequence of the efficiency and economy of the machine. This is a mental world strongly reminiscent of those of Alexander Calder, Man Ray, Jean Tinguely and Charles Eames. It is typical of these artists that they admire each other's thinking and results. Munari and his friend Calder openly referred to Man Ray as their inspiration; when, in 1954, Jean Tinguely made his meta-mechanical sculptures, he declared to have been inspired by Munari and, in his turn, Charles Eames also expressed admiration for the Italian. This was first clear of course in Eames' *Solar do Nothing Machine*, with which, in a similar way as Munari, he discussed the advantages over the profitability of the machine. Eames also literally expresses his respect. In a conversation with architect Gio Ponti, in which the latter openly voiced his admiration for the work of Eames and the American design world, Eames dryly responded by saying 'but you have Munari'.

Timo de Rijk

Bruno Munari was born on October 24th 1907 in Milan and died on September 30th 1998

Selected works

Pennellessa, 1970

While fantasy, invention, and creativity produce something that didn't exist before, imagination can also imagine something that already exists but that at the moment is not with us; imagination isn't necessarily creative. There are even cases in which the imagination fails to visualize a fantastic thought. Let's take an example: let's try to imagine a wooden motorcycle: the imagination can do this. You could also imagine a glass motorcycle, a completely transparent motorcycle (like those models of the human body in which you can see all the organs). But if you pass from solid material to liquid material and think of a liquid motorcycle... you can't visualize this, no matter how hard the imagination tries. Think of how many people see a face in the moon. Why only a face? Why not a peacock? A dung beetle? Because the dung beetle is never seen, it's not present in people's minds and therefore it's not recognized, while the human face is the first thing that a person sees on seeing the world. It's the first image that's committed to memory, that everyone memorizes, and therefore to say that you see a face in the moon is among the simplest connections that you can make. What do we see in the stains on walls, in the fragments of marble that make up certain pavements, in certain rocks, in certain clouds? Often a face. Someone sees a whale that is transformed into a camel.

Bruno Munari

The remake

We only had a very little low quality image (in the Bruno Munari, Air Made Visible book) of this magnificent object and asked ourselves, can we remake it? We tried. First buy the correct painters brush.

The brush must have long hairs (from horses tale), and buy some beautiful silk textile strip. Try to make the two pigtails. It will not be easy and you need 'one second contact glue'.

"The greatest obstacle to understanding a work of art is trying too hard." BM

Falkland Tubular lamp, 1964

Hyperbolic distortions of the cover that result from its elasticity, the changes in the cross-section are reminiscent of bamboo.

"The form is born spontaneously, in this case, from experimentation with materials and tensions. The rings are so disposed that light, placed above, can penetrate all the way to the bottom of the form, creating moiré patterns when you look through the layers of the mesh."

"One could also say a natural form: nature, in fact, creates its forms according to material, use, function, environment – simple forms like a drop of water, or more complicated forms like the praying mantis, all, however, made according to laws of constructive economy. In a bamboo cane the thickness of the material, the decreasing diameter, its elasticity, the disposition of knots, all respond to precise economic laws: wider at the top and narrower at the bottom would be a mistake; more rigid and it would break, more elastic and it would not support the weight of snow. All construction errors are not to be found in the aesthetic of thinks, but rather in the natural logical technique of construction. Consequently, it seems that an exact thing may also be beautiful to whomever studies it, and the observation of natural spontaneous forms can be very helpful to the designer accustomed to using materials for their nature, for their technical characteristics, and not using iron where wood would be better or glass where plastic would be better."

Bruno Munari

"The designer is therefore the artist of today, not because he is a genius but because he works in such a way as to re-establish contact between art and the public, because he has the humility and ability to respond to whatever demand is made of him by the society in which he lives." BM

Machine for seeing dawn before anyone else, 1942

Have someone give you an old alarm clock (1) and tie a strong thread (2) to the clapper. Set the clock and the alarm to the exact time given by the latest weather report. When the clapper vibrates it will move the nail file (3) back and forth.

The latter, kept horizontal by a fake zebra bone (4) that serves as a weight, will file the rod (5) supporting the horizontal board (6). This will slowly incline downwards. Luigi Occhio from Catania, asleep on the board, wishes naturally enough to be the first to see the dawn. Luigi (7) slips and drops right into the big wicker basket (8). As Luigi drops erect into the basket, the balloon (9) will by sheer change float into the sky.

Bruno Munari

Note:

a: You will have undoubtedly have read the article in Tuesday's newspaper which said; 'fatally wounded while cleaning the revolver he thought it was unloaded'. Well the wounded person was Luigi Occhi, 19, in person. Second lieutenant, third on the right, who – according to the article – was cleaning his gun, yesterday around three, when his mother came into the room on the tips of her slippers. A violent argument had broken out intentionally the night before, because of a girl who had, unknowingly, lent two mother-of-pearl buttons to Luigi, who, questioned by his mother, was unable to explain the fact; once established in the room, on the tips of her slippers (black), as we have said, she threw a large vase of absolutely no value at him, hitting him on the back of his head and, it is true, causing a fatal wound. Luigi is said to be mending well and should be out of the hospital in a couple of hours. The revolver was, as correctly surmised, unloaded. Sorry for all the commas.

b: Our firm also applies equipment for seeing the sunset after everybody else.

Bruno Munari

"The comic machines were projects for strange constructions for wagging the tails of lazy dogs, for predicting the dawn, for making sobs sound musical, and many other facetious things of that kind." BM

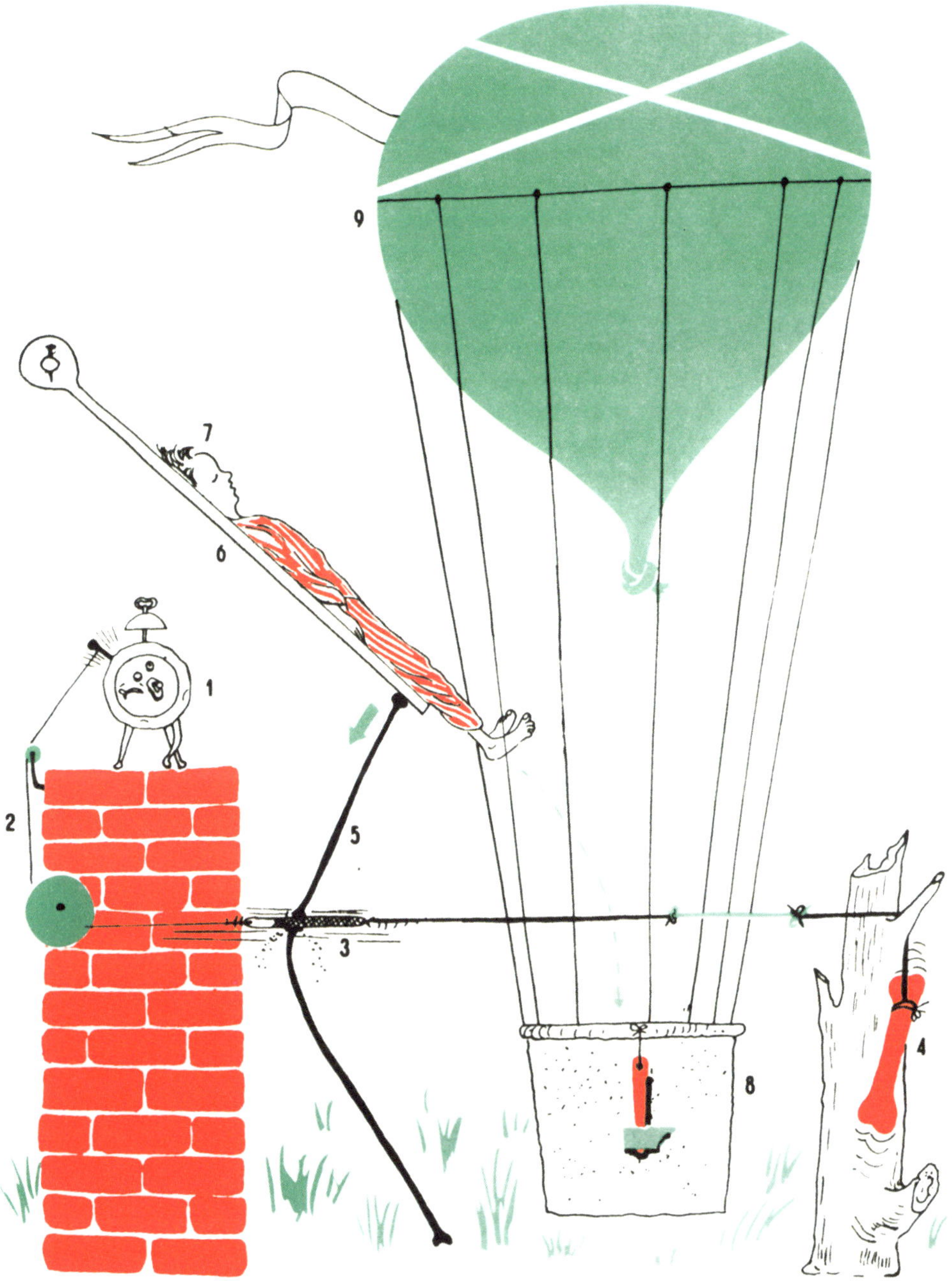
1
2
3
4
5
6
7
8
9

Useless machine, 1948

Wooden balls, metal wire, height 62 cm
Since 1933 Bruno Munari worked on 'useless machines'.

"The name 'useless machine' lends itself to many interpretations. The author considered these objects machines because they were made of various self-connected moving parts, and also because the famous lever (which is no more than a bar made of iron or wood or some other material) is a machine, even if only of the first degree. 'Useless' because they do not aid the creation of capital. Some people held that they were extremely useful, in fact, because they produce spiritual consumer goods (images, aesthetic sensibility, education of taste, kinetic information, and so on)."

"But how my friends laughed, even those whom I respected most for the care that they put into their work. Almost everybody had one of my useless machines in their house, which they kept in their children's rooms because it was considered a ridiculous and trifling thing, while they kept sculptures of Marino Marini and the paintings of Carra and Sironi in the living room. Certainly, in comparison with a painting of Sironi, where you saw the lion's claw, I with my cardboard and silk thread could not be taken seriously."

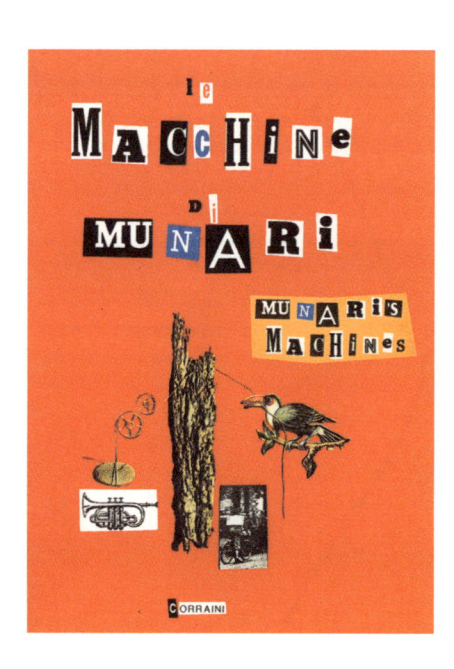

Bruno Munari

"Some people declared that the useless machines were extremely useful because they produced goods of a spiritual kind (images, aesthetic sense, the cultivation of taste, kinetic information, etc.)." BM

41 BRIGHT MINDS, BEAUTIFUL IDEAS

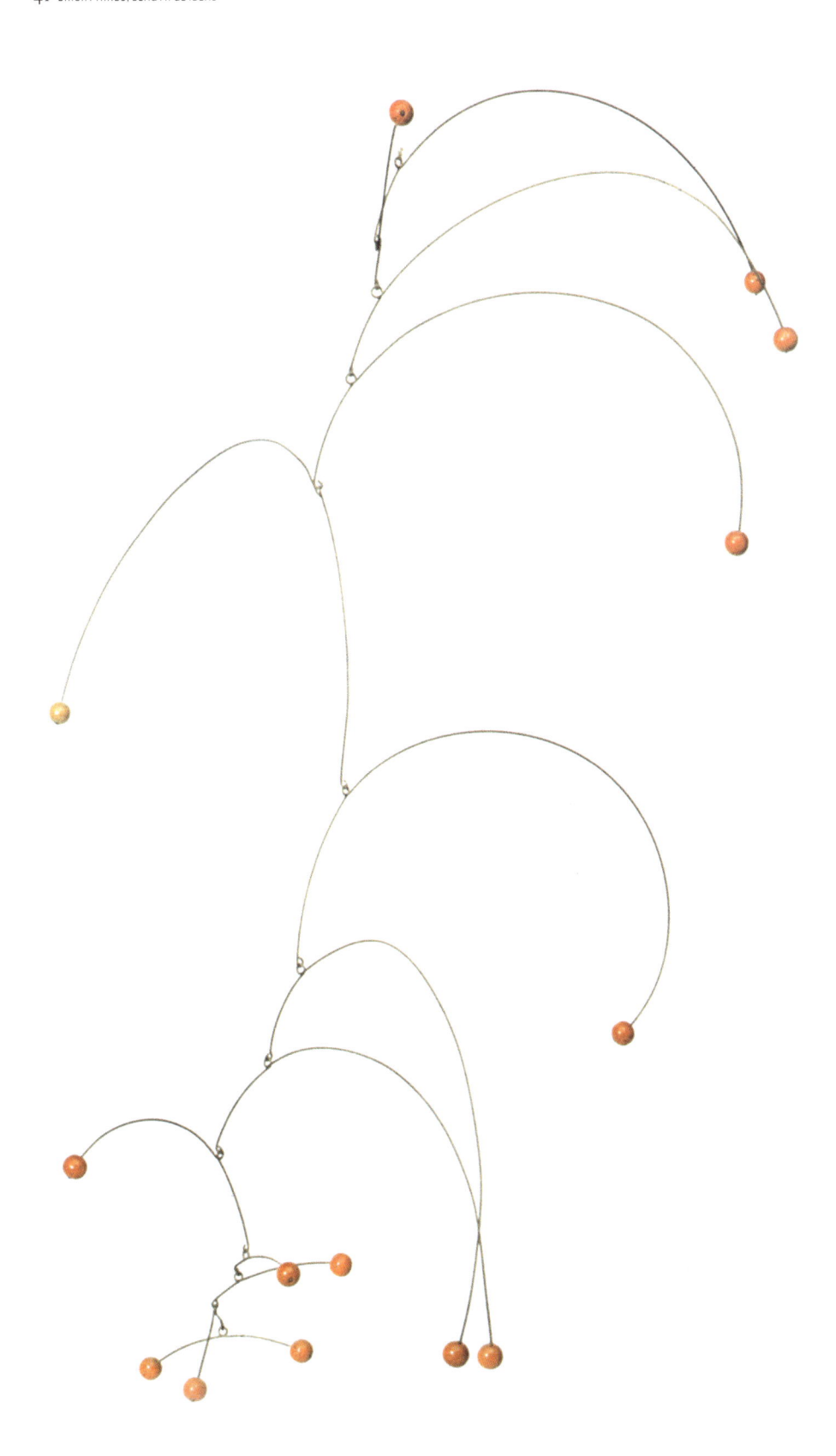

Seeking comfort in an uncomfortable chair, ca. 1950
Bruno Munari in a sequence of photographs.

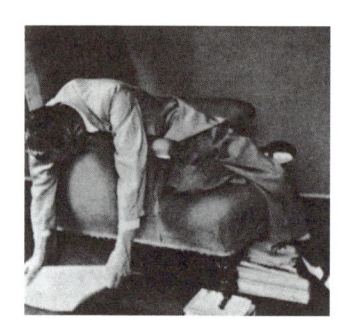

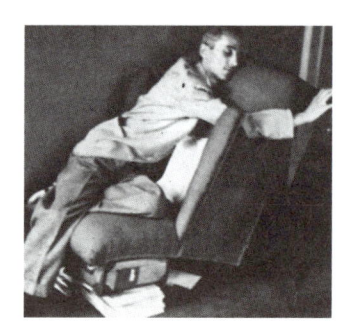

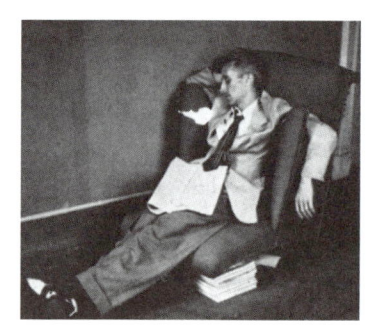

"Making things complicated is easy. Achieving simplicity is tough." BM

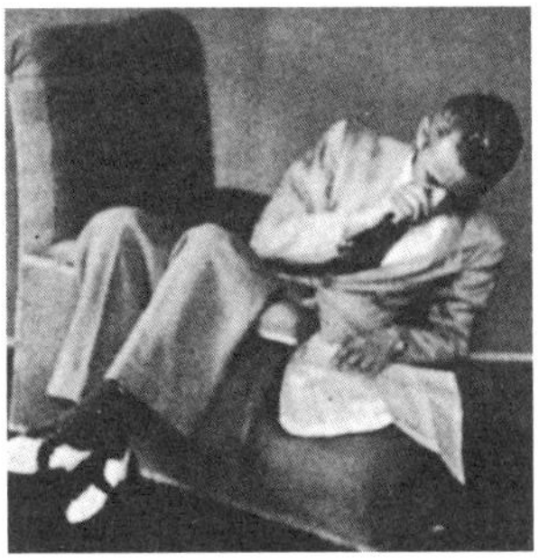
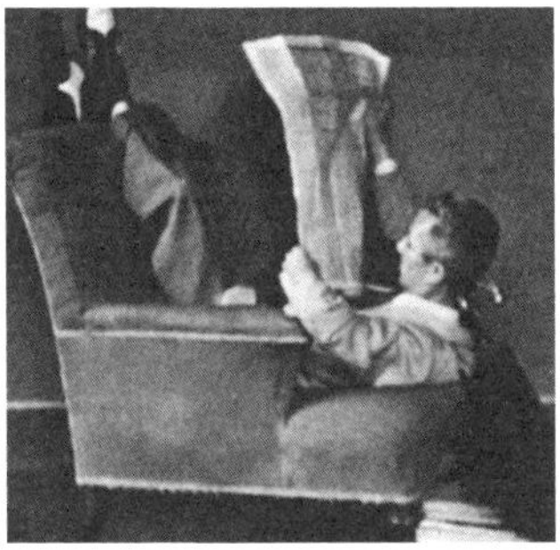
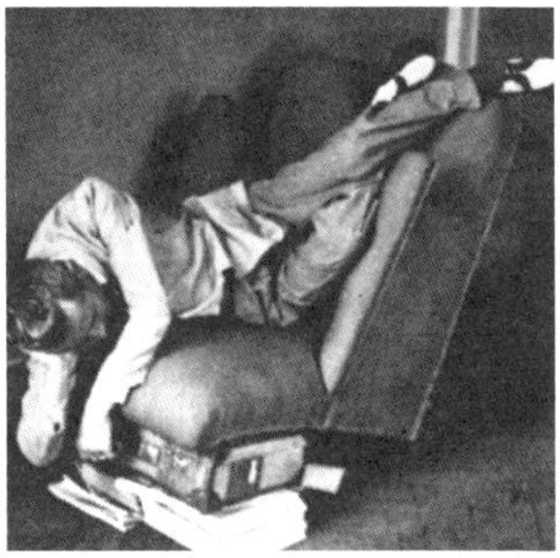
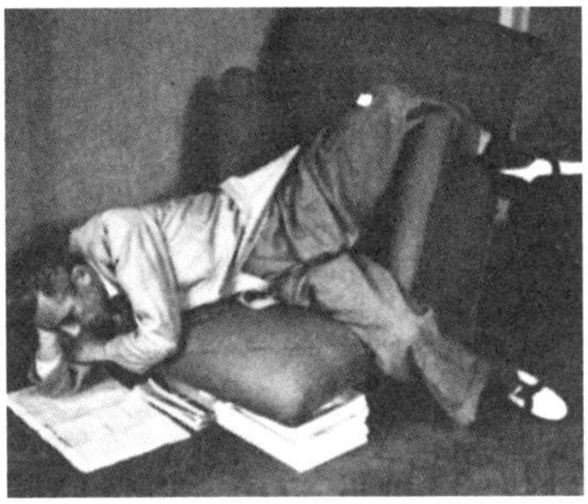
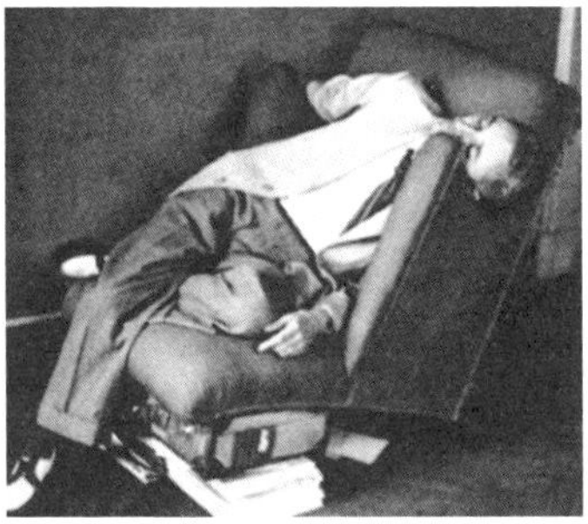
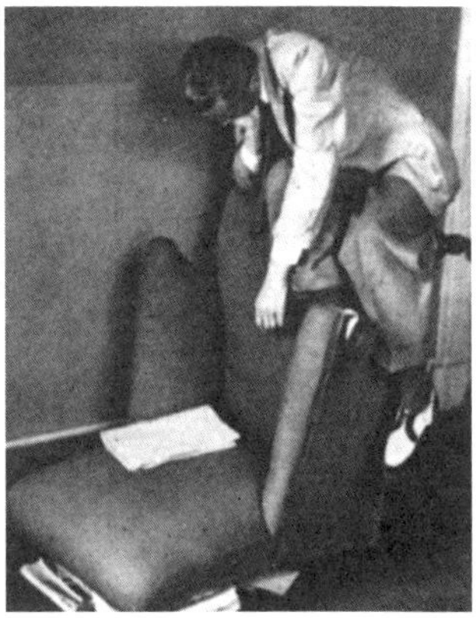

The foam-rubber cat has nylon claws, 1949
For Pirelli

'When a cat is soft, smooth, and clean, when it can be put in a wide variety of postures in which it will then stay put, when it doesn't go pee pee anywhere, when it doesn't require any care, when it doesn't have to be fed, and when it, let's say, also has nylon claws-what more can you ask?'

I would really like to speed up the manufacturing process, but how can I do that in the enormously expansive industrial complex of Pirelli as big as its own country, where important interests are involved. Me, Bruno Munari, weighing just 48 kilos, I do not see myself as someone who could disturb all this activity, and so I wait for my cat, out front on the street corner, together with two lost children who have asked if they can have it for Christmas.

Bruno Munari in Pirelli's corporate magazine.

"Anyone who uses a properly designed object feels the presence of an artist who has worked for him, bettering his living conditions and encouraging him to develop his taste and sense of beauty." BM

Unreadable book, 1953

For Steendrukkerij De Jong & Co in Hilversum, the Netherlands. Made of red and white paper.

"The goal of this experiment is to see if it is possible to use the materials that make up a book (excluding the text) as a visual language. The problem is this: can you communicate visually and tactilely only by means of editorial production of a book? Or can the book as object communicate something independently of the printed words? And if so, what?"

"Normally, books are made with just a few types of paper and are bound in two or three different styles. The paper is used to support the text and illustrations, and not as something communicable."

Bruno Munari

Munari's forks, 1958

"These variations on the fork, indeed on the fork as an 'extension' of the hand (and, finally, as the hand), were drawn without any practical aim, rather to allow the imagination to play on an apparently arid theme, on the order of a typically European structural problem, as the foundation for a language that guarantees recovery."

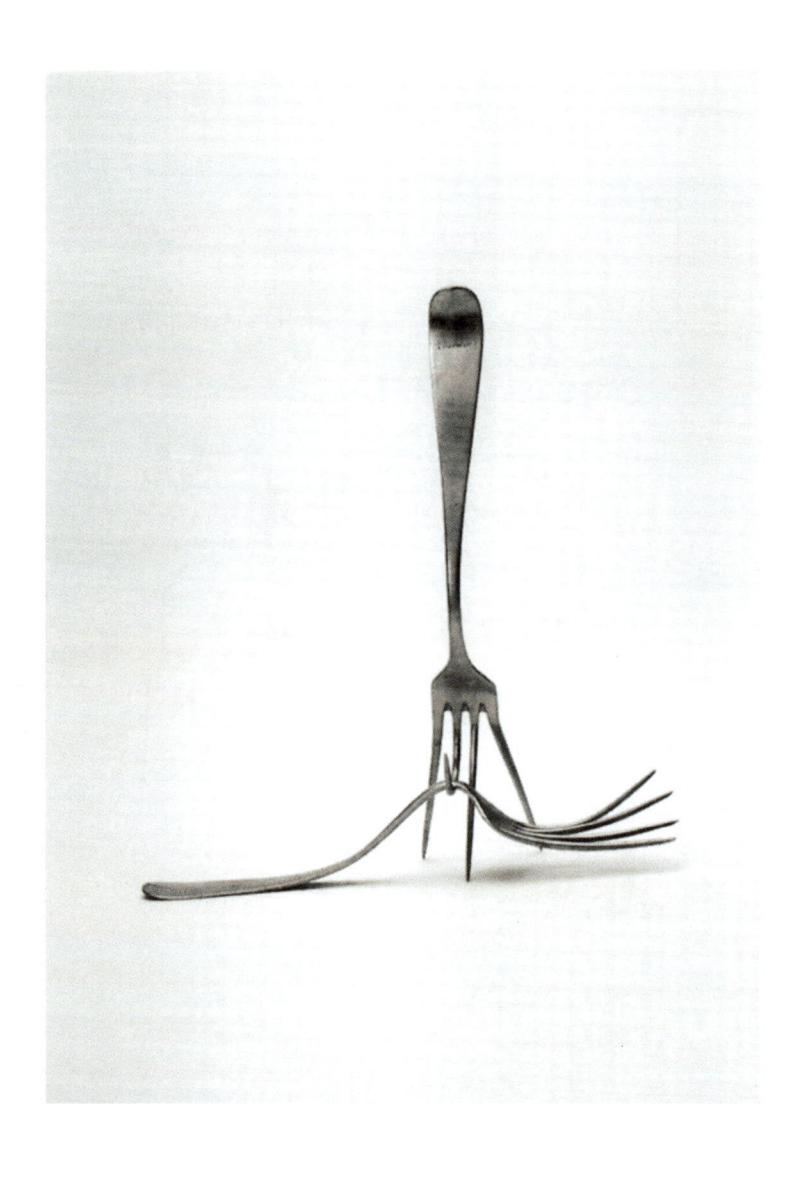

Bruno Munari

Da lontano era un'isola, 1938

Have you ever tried to line up several stones – the kind with a white stripe? On the beach at Baratti, together with some children, we made one of these stripes, of striped stones, traversing the sand from the water to the shrubbery – like a border between two zones of the beach. Then we sat down to watch the people's reactions; only a few people even noticed the stripe; some stepped over it without looking; others kicked some of the stones; a dog stopped to sniff them. The next day it was partially destroyed.

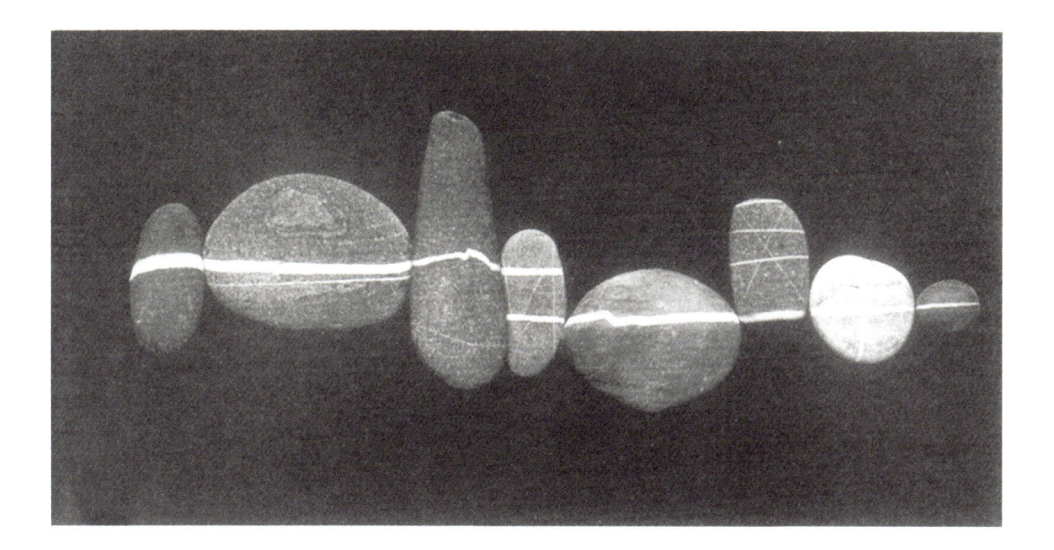

Bruno Munari

"Change is born of the climate, of ambient conditions, social, geographic, of sensory receptions. A smell of eucalyptus, the shape of a stone, the rhythm of ocean waves..." BM

Anonymous products

Bruno Munari collected his whole life 'anonymous products' from over the globe. As an inspirational source for design students and designers this collection travels as exhibition worldwide.

This collection anonymous products by Bruno Munari was awarded with the *'Il Compasso D'oro'* for 'the anonymous designer' at the Triennial in Milan.

'Il Compasso d'Oro' (The Golden Compass Award). This prize, first awarded in 1954, aims to acknowledge and promote quality in the field of industrial designs Made in Italy and is awarded by ADI (Associazione Design Industriale). ADI is an association of 750 manufacturers, as well as the most capable architects and designers in Italy.

Timeline 1919-1971

What was happening in the world in the years Bruno Munari and Charles & Ray Eames were active.
We made a selection of influential political events, happenings, discoveries and inventions.

Timeline 1919-1971

1919: Walter Gropius founds the Bauhaus in Weimar.
1920: Mahatma Gandhi begins non-violent campaign against British colonialist rule.
1921: Partition of Ireland. In China the Communist Party is established, in Germany the National Socialist German Workers Party (NSDAP). Nobel Prize in Physics for Albert Einstein.
1922: With Mussolini's march to Rome fascism starts in Italy.
1923: End of Ottoman State, Republic of Turkey proclaimed by Kemal Atatürk. Hitler putsch in Munich. Founding of the Soviet-Union. First experimental sound movies in US.
1924: Lenin dies, Stalin rules. First small film camera (Leica). Rietveld-Schröder House.
1925: 'Mein Kampf' is published.
1926: 'Metropolis' by Fritz Lang, and the first Mickey Mouse movie.
1927: Charles Lindbergh crosses the Ocean with his plane. First fabrication of PVC in the US and Germany. First television broadcasts in England.
1928: Penicillin discovered. First television on sale in America.
1929: October 29th is Black Friday at the New York Stock Exchange. The World Economic Crisis. Airship Zeppelin flies around the world.
1930: Invention photo flashlight. First World Cup Championship of football. First radio.
1931: Many investors go bankrupt when investing in the Empire State Building.
1932: Worldwide depression and unemployment.
1933: Hitler takes over power in Germany.
1934: 'The Long March' by Mao Zedong in China. Magnetron invented.
1935: Radar and nylon invented.
1936: Standard Oil finds oil in the desert of Saudi Arabia.
1937: Civil war in Spain, general Franco takes power. Picasso paints 'Guernica'.
1938: Munich Pact. Uranium atom divided.
1939: Germany invades Poland despite non-attack pact; Russia joins in and both countries divide the country. France and GB declare war. USSR invades Finland.
1940: Hitler takes Holland, Belgium and France.
1941: Japanese attack at Pearl Harbor means American involvement in World War II.
1942: Start 'Profit Boom': involvement in the war boosts American economy.
1943: 'Le petit Prince' by Antoine de Saint-Exupéry is published.
1944: Paris and Rome liberated. D-Day in Normandy.
1945: Atom bomb on Hiroshima and Nagasaki. With the Yalta conference the Cold War starts. United Nations founded.
1946: Benjamin Spock's 'The common sense book of baby and child care' is published.
1947: Start Marshall plan. India independent.
1948: The United Nations adopt and proclaim the Universal Declaration of Human Rights. The Kinsey Report about sexual behavior in the Human Male, stating that 10% is homosexual, heralds a new, more progressive era.
1949: Foundation of the Sate Israel.
1950: American invasion pushes North Korean troops out of South Korea.
1951: Computers are first sold commercially in the US.
1953: Stalin dies.
1954: First successfully completed kidney transplant in the US.
1955: Ray Kroc opens the first MacDonald's Restaurant in Des Plaines.
1956: Elvis scores three number one hits. Crisis in the Middle East about Suez Canal. Cuban Revolution. Video recorder invented.
1957: The USSR launches the first satellite Sputnik.
1958: European Parliament established. Photocopier invented.
1959: During 'The Moscow Kitchen Debate' Richard Nixon and Nikita Khrushchev talk politics in an Eames kitchen. In London 'The teenage consumer' about youth culture comes out. Microchip invented.

1960: Laser beam invented in the United States. Mao officially declares 'The Great Leap forward' was an economic disaster.
1961: Start construction of Berlin Wall. Yuri Gagarin is the first human to pilot a spacecraft.
1962: The Cuban Missile Crisis almost leads to an atomic war. First James Bond Movie: Dr No.
1963: John F. Kennedy murdered. Betty Friedman's, 'The Feminine Mystique' comes out. Computer mouse Invented.
1964: Nobel Prize for Martin Luther King.
1965: President Johnson starts large-scale American intervention in Vietnam.
1967: First heart transplant in South Africa.
1968: Summer of love. Martin Luther King murdered. Russians invade Czechoslovakia. '2001, a space Odyssey' by Stanley Kubrick.
1969: Woodstock. Neil Armstrong lands on the moon. US and the Soviet Union sign the Nuclear Non-Proliferation Treaty. First video recorder for sale. ARPA-net, the first Internet, started.
1970: Vietnam-war spreads to Laos and Cambodia. Crisis in the Middle East. Salvador Allende becomes president of Chili. The Beatles break up, rock guitarist Jimi Hendrix dies at age 27.
1971: Floppydisk and microprocessor invented.

Charles & Ray Eames

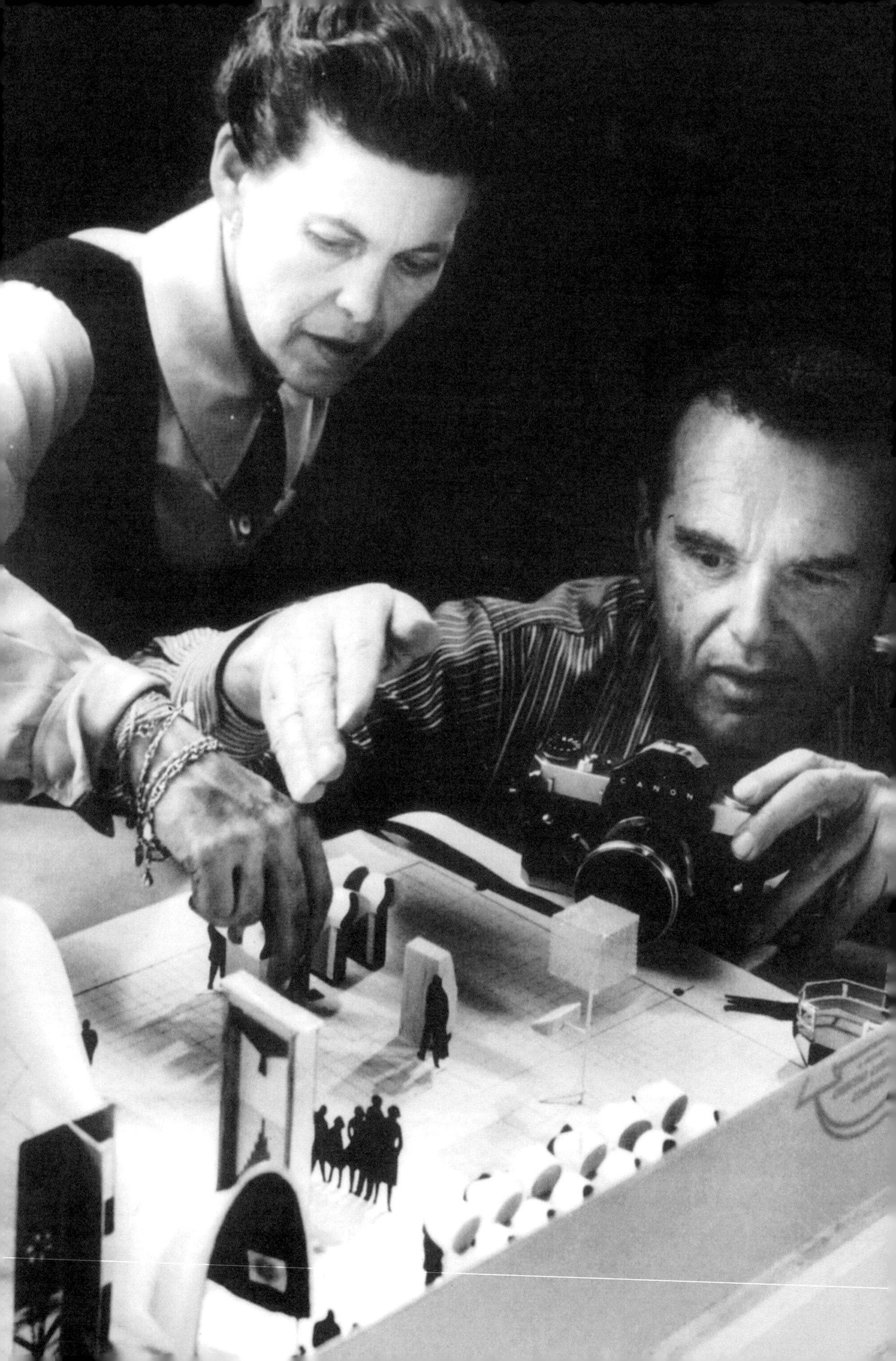
CANON

Charles & Ray Eames

Eames and Eames

Ray (1912-1988) and Charles (1907-1978) Eames designed many of the design icons of the last century. Even people who do not know their name, know their work, or might even sit on one of their world famous chairs in their home or office. As designers the couple are legendary. Every designer wants to be at least a little like the Eameses. Design luminaries like Terence Conran, Jasper Morisson and Aldo van Eyck rate their work among the finest and most important product design of the twentieth century and stress the major impact it has had on their lives.

At the same time it is this immense regard for their furniture designs that is partly to blame for the bad name which the concept of design and the profession of designer has at this time. The fact is the work of the Eameses personifies the representative side of design – the status it bestows on multinationals, lawyers and anyone else who can afford the highly priced soft pad and lounge chairs to decorate their boardrooms and offices like trophies of good taste. A wry paradox is the acceptance of work by designers who dedicated themselves to having modern, mass-produced products recognised and actually promoted affordable modern furniture for everyone. During his own lifetime, Charles Eames was already aware of this dangerous sting in his own design tail. On one of his early trips to Europe in the early fifties, during a visit to a department store that had his furniture in its collection, he came to the appalling conclusion that his chairs were being sold at ten times the price they were in America. Much later, when it was already evident that his designs were also sold as status symbols, to the question of whether design was for the masses, the wealthy or specialists, he gave the meaningful reply: 'design is addressed to the need'.

The designer's role

Charles and Ray Eames were clear about their intentions when designing products – they ought to improve the world. In itself in the 1930s – the formative years of Charles Eames and Ray Kaiser – this was not anything unusual, at least not in the world of the European avant-garde. But it certainly was for a young American architect like Charles Eames, who at first was still barely aware of such a tradition.

Eames was a talented architect for whom during the 1930s nothing stood in the way of further building on a career as a successful designer of comfortable, modern Georgian villas for well-paying clients in the Midwest. A meeting with the pre-eminent immigrant architect Eliel Saarinen and his son Eero was the first to change all that. The Cranbrook Academy, where Saarinen taught and Eames studied, was one of the few places in America where a similar European avant-garde belief had been able to gain a foothold. Here, along with Saarinen, the idealistic European tradition, largely absent elsewhere in the country, had established itself. After his meeting with Saarinen, Eames questioned – probably for the first time – his role as a designer. Did he want more than unique designs for houses and churches? Was he happy with the conventional relationship between architect and client, and if not, what should it then be like? At first he was at an utter loss with such questions and uncertainty, even though he was impressed with Saarinen's work and the stories of his son, who almost immediately became a lifelong friend.

The breakthrough came shortly afterwards in 1940 when he met the artist Ray Kaiser. Kaiser had studied painting in New York – like Cranbrook one of the few places where modern European artistic ideas could be found. It was she, with her defiant views on modern European painting, that inspired Eames to find and take up an independent position within his field. Raising the issue of the everyday job of designer, which until then Eames had practised with satisfaction and without any doubts whatsoever, was at the time an unexpected and by no means obvious step. While modern art may have been continually preoccupied with its rights to exist, a similar standpoint for architecture and design, especially in America, was far less self-evident. America was certainly familiar with avant-garde artists – in the 1930s they often made the newspapers and magazines namely as 'curiosities', but similar examples in the design world hardly existed as yet. At the same time, the fertile world of exhibitions, debate, publications and clients based around architecture and design was completely absent there.

The road to paradise
Together Charles and Ray, with great dedication, searched and found a role for design in the avant-garde movement. But what had they thought they would find? After the Depression, which took its greatest toll on America in 1929, the country quickly struggled to its feet and by the mid-thirties America was the pre-eminent land of consumerism. During the Depression in America, designers precisely for economic reasons, had set to work and in the 1930s window-dressers, set designers and teachers of drawing retrained as designers for industry. Professional design was used as commercial persuader – American designers came up with new unique selling points often for old existing products. Charles had experienced the birth of this new profession from close by in fact. However, he decided not to be associated with this well-paid line of business. Once with Ray, he saw ever more clearly the huge disadvantages of burgeoning consumerism in the thick mail order catalogues and the endless assortment of goods in the major department stores. It was not so much the scale of the number of products, but the sheer overwhelming choice on offer that swamped American society. The Eameses did not have an immediate alternative at the ready, but continued to have a deeply felt awareness that American consumers were waiting to be 'liberated' from the products and attendant ideas from grandmother's time. Note, however, that for the Eameses, in sharp contrast to the European avant-garde, modern design was not in the first instance a solution for hunger, unhygienic conditions and a lack of housing. For both Charles and Ray it was the fact that as modern designers they wanted to deliver American buyers from products with imposed considerations of status. Both had a clear-cut image of the disadvantages of American culture – to which serious shortcomings like hunger and deprivation obviously belonged – but which in their eyes were chiefly personified in the artificial gloss many designers and manufacturers applied to their products. This spurious gloss manifested itself in an exaggerated predilection for luxury, especially imitation, which gave working class people the sense that they possessed something from the upper classes: a sofa in the form of a Buick, a car with the look of an aircraft or a mock Versailles cupboard. According to the Eameses such products held back the development of the real mental freedom of the consumers. Their objective was, in the most modern sense of the term, the 'democratisation' of the object.
With this type of 'democratised' design, the couple had in mind the social and cultural liberation of the Americans in highly concrete terms, even though that goal was not devoid of self-interest. Ray Eames articulated this very clearly when she recalled memories of early discussions with her late husband. At the time he was designing his first items of furniture with his friend Eero Saarinen, who had set him on the path of a modern, almost classless furniture style, which in his case meant an undecorated design bereft of historical references. Through Ray, Charles realised that every new design for the same kind of product required the same kind of effort each time. A chair was followed by a second and a third, with the enormous danger that the wish to design and unnecessary originality during the design process would gain the upper hand. The Eameses decided that a once-only, all-out effort necessary to make the perfect chair should suffice, and at the same time produce a result that would benefit as many users as possible.

In practice
These were fine words and interesting ideas. Charles and Ray Eames were to learn the answers to their crucial questions on accessibility and acceptance of their designs in practise. The year 1940 provided a good opportunity. The curator, Eliot Noyes, from New York's Museum of Modern Art wrote out a competition entitled 'Organic

Furniture' to find designs for affordable furniture. Like the Saarinens, Noyes was extremely well informed about all the latest developments in the world of avant-garde design. After experimenting with tubular steel, many designers, especially those from Scandinavia, were attempting to design a more congenial version of mass produced wooden chairs and other furniture designs. At that point, the work of the Finnish designer Alvar Aalto was among the leading mature experiments in the field, and Noyes invited him to sit on the jury panel. Under Aalto's direction, two submissions from Eames and Saarinen were awarded first prize. The prize-winning plywood chairs had a distinctive fluent design and bore all the promise of mass production. And although they looked somewhat clumsy, they were instantly spotted throughout America.

While it had been Noyes's express intention to reach a wider public with affordable, mass-produced furniture, this ideal still seemed a long way off. During the exhibition, Noyes, at the time ashamed and annoyed by his director, wrote: 'the excitement of sitting in them is not going to be a middle class thrill at this point because prices are something terrific'. Despite the Eameses good intentions of 'enlightened' design gaining broad acceptance, their efforts were destined to fulfil an honorary role within high culture from the MoMA depot.

The couple saw the danger and did everything in their power to get industrial production of their furniture from the ground. Various circumstances came to their aid. In the first place Bloomingdale's department store was prepared – no doubt with broad approval from the designers – to sell their prize-winning designs at cost price, an unprecedented gesture in America's commercial world. The premise looked favourable – until America also became engaged in the Second World War. Within a few weeks following the attack on Pearl harbour (July 1941), the Eameses were not allowed to use rubber, metal and plywood for their experimental furniture production. The ambitious couple were forced to suspend their quest for socially motivated design.

Immediately following the outbreak of war, the cultural world was also called to make a contribution to the war effort. Along with other artists, Charles and Ray Eames were enlisted for a cultural war programme aimed at making maximum use of America's artistic talent. Many painters and sculptors were employed to make propaganda material, while Charles Eames himself was given a dream commission. His knowledge of plywood – still limited at the time – was used to make military material, especially for the airforce. Aircraft builders acquainted him with various production techniques and possibilities, which up until then he had only experimented with using cheap materials in the spare room of his Santa Monica apartment. In immense factories useful cockpit chairs, wings, fuselage and entire aircraft from wood were now made. During the war the possibilities to bend, mould and glue were combined with the need for a huge industrial production. Eames saw his chance, especially when he heard that certain products in the war functioned extremely badly. A friend drew his attention to metal stretchers and splints in use by the American marines. These items were heavy and thus so dangerous when in use that according to reports they had even cost lives. Eames saw the possibility to use his fascination for plywood and his limited experience of mass production gained with companies to make a really 'socially engaged' product – the plywood splint. Its strong, light construction and flexibility were ideal for mass-production. Never before had the experience of making a socially relevant object been so forceful. The awareness of the social necessity of design was never to leave the Eamses.

Design as art: an apparent contradiction
Within a few years Charles and Ray Eames had changed from artists to social engineers – designers who first thought about the place and function of products rather than the form and style of the products themselves. For Charles, the transition was a big step, but also for Ray, who had been raised with the concept of visionary artistry. Together with Charles, Ray was now the avant-garde of social design. Due to the Second World War, both artists and designers in the entire western world felt the need for a new legitimacy. Where the question of social relevance before the war had been chiefly a matter for a small avant-garde – sometimes insufferable to a wider public, it was now the concern of everyone. And only rarely could the question be answered with the cry l'art pour l'art (art for art's sake).

Now the roles appeared to be reversed. Instantly activities like weaving, pottery, glassblowing and silversmithing were seen as suspect and even unethical activties, which the old social relationships deemed dangerous occupations. Certainly in design circles, industrial design, with its highly utilitarian notion, served as the guiding principle by which many designers worked – and then no longer to produce luxury or imitation luxury goods, but to find practical and user-friendly solutions for everyday problems. The lonely artist was suspected of being an elitist and anti-socially engaged. It was no small wonder that Eames continually rebelled against his lifelong 'genius' label, bestowed on him by so many.

Seen in this light, it is remarkable that the Eameses remained openly – and with complete conviction – interested in the visual arts and in craftsmanship, tradition and nostalgia. In the formulating of the new requirements for the social designer, they considered the dogmatic rejection of the 'irrational' would also lead to attractive and valuable attributes of this being lost. Furthermore, they felt that all these – unofficially forbidden – interests had unique qualities that were extremely important for designers. Adopting this attitude – viewed as a contradictory one at the time – they warned against the false certainty of one-sidedness, in the same way they did in the way they worked at their office, in their life at home and particularly in their design work. Even before the time they exchanged visionary artistry for the position of social designer, they knew art could look far and touch deeply. The statement by art dealer Sidney James, who once wrote about the group to which Ray Eames belonged, exactly expresses what the couple thought: 'As if by magic whole new worlds of the spirit are lit up, worlds of poetic interference, mythological worlds, worlds of haunting reminiscence, of unearthly fantasy and disquieting dreams'. The social design task of the Eamses was not only a simple calculation of material wishes and necessities. For them their fondness for playfulness, poetry and association were just as important as well as – not to forget – the almost absurd and even nostalgic aspects of design. Years later when Ray Eames gave an account of their office in a book, the first thing she showed was the machine that produced the first plywood chairs. Thus, according to her, the history of the office began with an experiment. From the beginning, Charles and Ray Eames combined that desirable avant-garde trademark with the innovation of the engineer and designer.

The Eames culture and progress

Charles and Ray Eames understood better than anyone that culture in the western world is a paradox in itself. Culture is by definition a combination of assumptions and unconscious ideas that change very slowly. But one of these fixed ideas in both Europe and certainly in America is a strong belief in progress, a predilection for experimenting and innovation. In their work the couple reconciled these fixed views with the puritanical idea of progress – humanity as a measure of things, as the centrepoint that controls the environment and is continually searching for improvement in art and science. They reconciled tradition with experimentation and innovation, usefulness with enjoyment, apparent superficiality with timelessness. One of their finest commercial briefs was to produce a design for the future in which the possibilities of aluminium were shown to their best advantage. The Eames office invented the Solar Do-Nothing machine, a solar-panelled operating mobile comprising light-hearted and playful components. It is a charmingly animated, futuristic machine, which was considered so beautiful that no-one actually asked what it did. The object was typical of Charles and Ray Eames. In one of Charles's early designs, the leg splint from 1941, he combined Surrealism with association and the ghastly need of a functioning product. In the Solar Do-Nothing machine the couple combined technical innovation with the most engaging form of uselessness. And to quote Charles Eames: 'Who is to say that pleasure is useless'.

Timo de Rijk

Charles Eames was born on June 17th 1907, St Louis, Missouri, U.S.A. Died August 21st 1978.

Ray Eames: Alexandra Kaiser was born 1912 California, U.S.A. Died August 21st 1988.

"One can't look at a project without thinking of the next smaller or larger thing"
Charles Eames

"Go to Disneyland"

In 1958, at the age of 17 Rolf Fehlbaum (Vitra) visited Charles Eames. On Rolf's question where to go to to understand the American culture Charles replied with "Go to Disneyland".

"Even Sunday school was not as valuable as being in nature, and we would just be out in the country."
Ray Eames Kaiser

"She has a very good sense of what gives an idea, or form, or piece of sculpture its character, of how its relationships are formed. She can see when there is a wrong mix of ideas or materials, where the division between two ideas isn't clear. If this sounds like a structural or architectural idea, it is."
Charles Eames

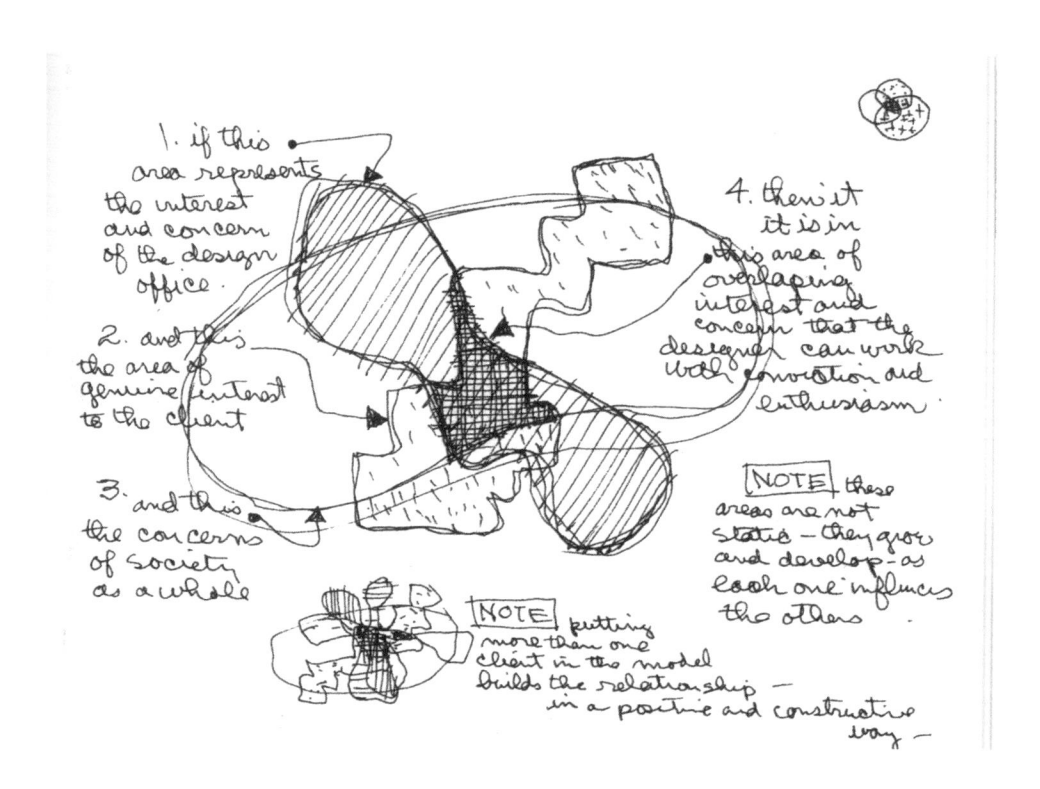

"It is not that I'm embarrassed about 'designer' so much as the degree to which I prefer the word 'architect' and what it implies. It implies structure, a kind of analysis, as well as a kind of tradition behind it."
Charles Eames

Selected works

Leg splint, 1941

This project started in 1941 when Ray and Charles were informed about problems with metal leg splints used in the military. These metal splints did not support the injured leg well enough. The first production experiments with molded plywood leg splints took place in their newly rented space in Los Angeles. They initiated the Plyformed Wood Company that produced the first 5000 pcs. which were ordered by the Navy.

Giant house of cards, 1953

This set of cards is bigger then 'house of cards' and carries a more selective range of images. The images are according to the box label 'Colorful panels to build with – each with a graphic design taken from the arts – the sciences – the world around us'. The images including an architectural column, an engraving of snowflakes, a scroll of calligraphy, a classic letter construction, a blow-up of an egg shell, a mathematical model – were chosen from dozens of candidates as examples of the richness of our historical visual traditions of the world around us.

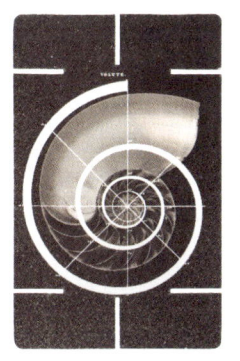

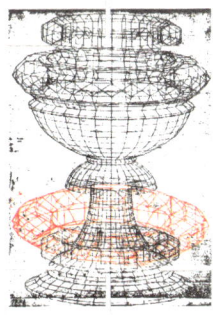

Wood-legged dining chair DCW, 1945
The goal was to produce an inexpensive, high quality chair using industrial technologies developed during the war. The assembly of the different plywood elements of this chair made it possible to replace a back or a seat which was seen as better than the lost of a complete chair. By experimenting with tools, materials and molds the Molded Plywood Division of Evan products in Venice, California in close co-operation with Ray and Charles invented a complete new and reliable production method.

A Communications primer, 1953

Charles Eames wanted this film to inspire greater appreciation of the broad meaning of 'communication' and to advocate the breakdown of barriers between various disciplines. The film was an Eames attempt to interpret and present current ideas on communications theory to architects and planners in an understandable way and to encourage their use as tools in planning and design. The first film production by the Eames office based on the communications theory outlined in the 1949 book 'The mathematical Theory of Communication' by Claude Shannon.

Molded plywood Animals, 1945

The experiments with molded plywood led to a group of animal toys. The animals were not produced; an existing marketing program could not be found, and Evans Products was not prepared at this point to set up a furniture distribution system.

It was characteristic of Charles to extend the concepts or technology of a major project to ideas that seemed to be merely tangential to the main problem. In later years, many of these lateral moves developed into projects, toys, and films that became important milestones in his work.

John Entenza (employee of the Eames office) and Ray wearing animal masks for an impromptu performance.

Alcoa Solar Do-Nothing Machine, 1957

For the promotion of aluminum the Eames office was asked to design an aluminum toy for the Aluminum Company of America. The approach was to investigate the use of solar energy in combination with lightweight, reflective properties of aluminum. After many months of experimentation with the cells, the office came up with the 'Solar Do-Nothing Machine', a device that converted sunlight into electrical energy to run motion displays. Although the machine 'did nothing' and was not a product to be marketed and sold, it provided an early working demonstration of potential union between aluminum and solar energy.

"Who is to say that pleasure is useless"
Charles Eames

House of cards, 1952

Charles and Ray's view of toys was never frivolous. There was always a point to be made and something to be learned by both adults and children. While the toys were appealing on a purely sensory level, a closer look revealed messages about the things human beings make and use and the everyday objects we take for granted but no longer see as useful and beautiful.

Charles Eames returned again and again, in toys, films, slide shows, and exhibitions, to the message that we only have to look at our immediate surroundings and the things we use and love for a deep and lasting appreciation of art in its truest form.

"Yes, almost everything that was ever collected was just because of an example of some facet of design and form. We never collected anything just as collectors, but because something was inherent in the piece that made it seem like a good idea to be looking at. Seashells, certainly. From early on we had chemical lab products, you know, containers, because the form was beautiful and pure and they were made of fine material and, at that time, were very inexpensive. We felt that was a great example. We had cereal bowls that were evaporating dishes and teacups that were made by the chemical people – a beautiful form. They're now unbelievably expensive because they were made by hand, but the form had been developed over many years. Charles believed in what was in one of the films – putting in what was good and taking out what was bad. Over the years, having a form developed."
Ray Eames Kaiser

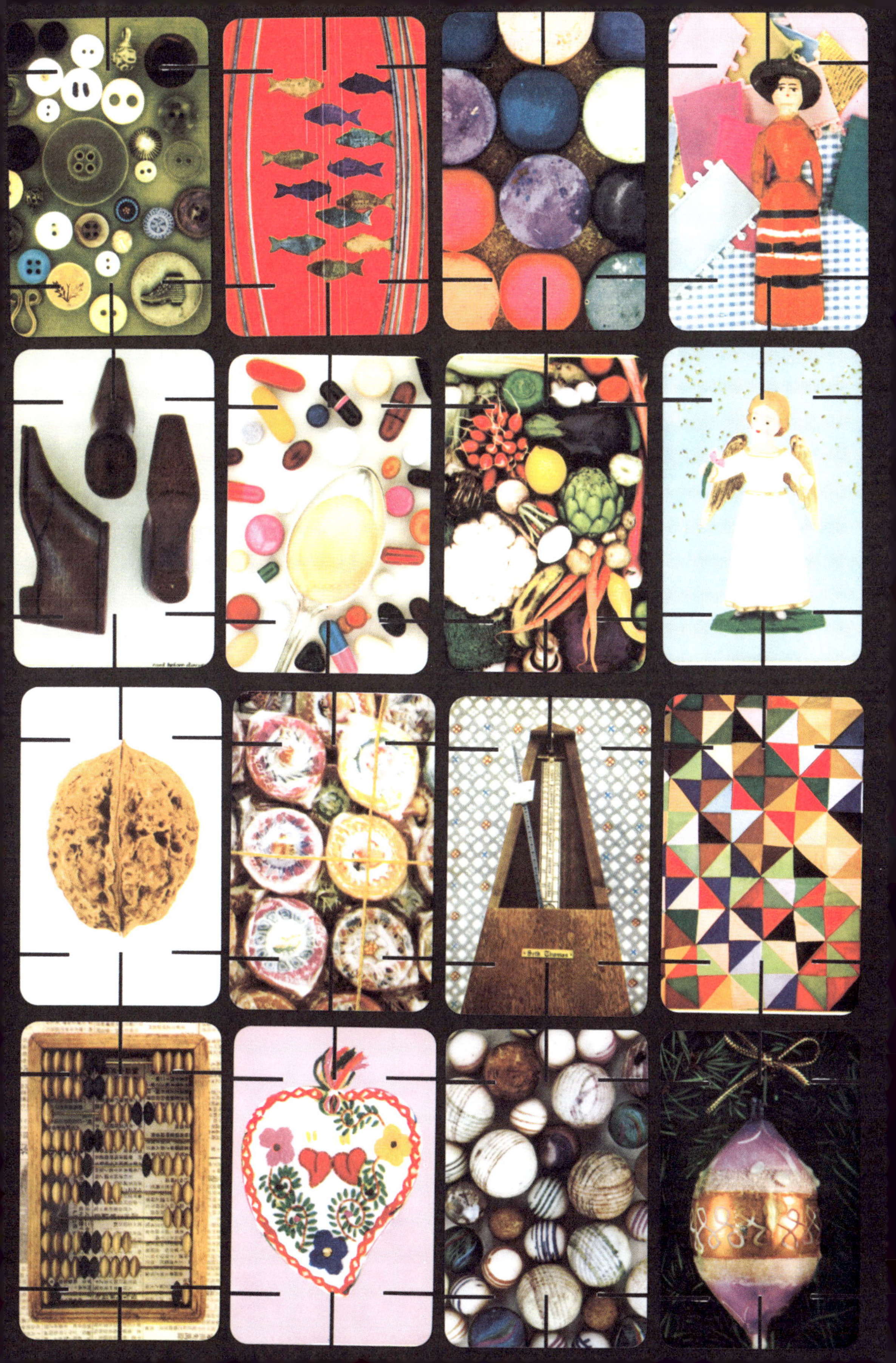
Seth Thomas

Film: Clown face, 1971
Bill Ballantine (director of the Clown College of Ringling brothers) approached Charles to provide him with 'a casual couple of hundred feet of film' that he could use in teaching clown make-up. The film that began as a tutorial on clown make-up became a twenty-minute film that is also an exercise in demonstrating the concept of symmetry, using the symmetry of the human face as its example.

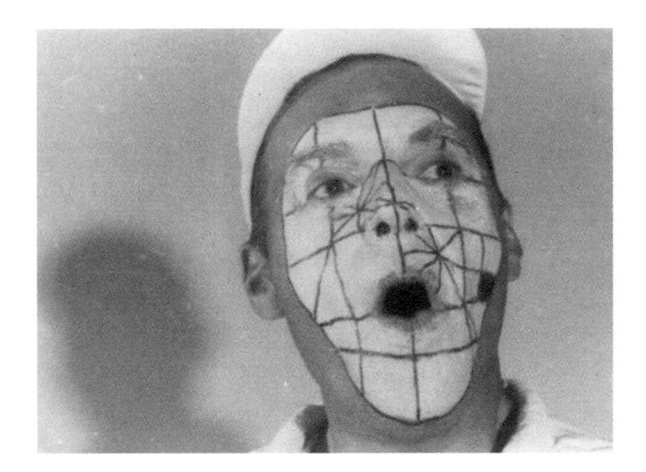

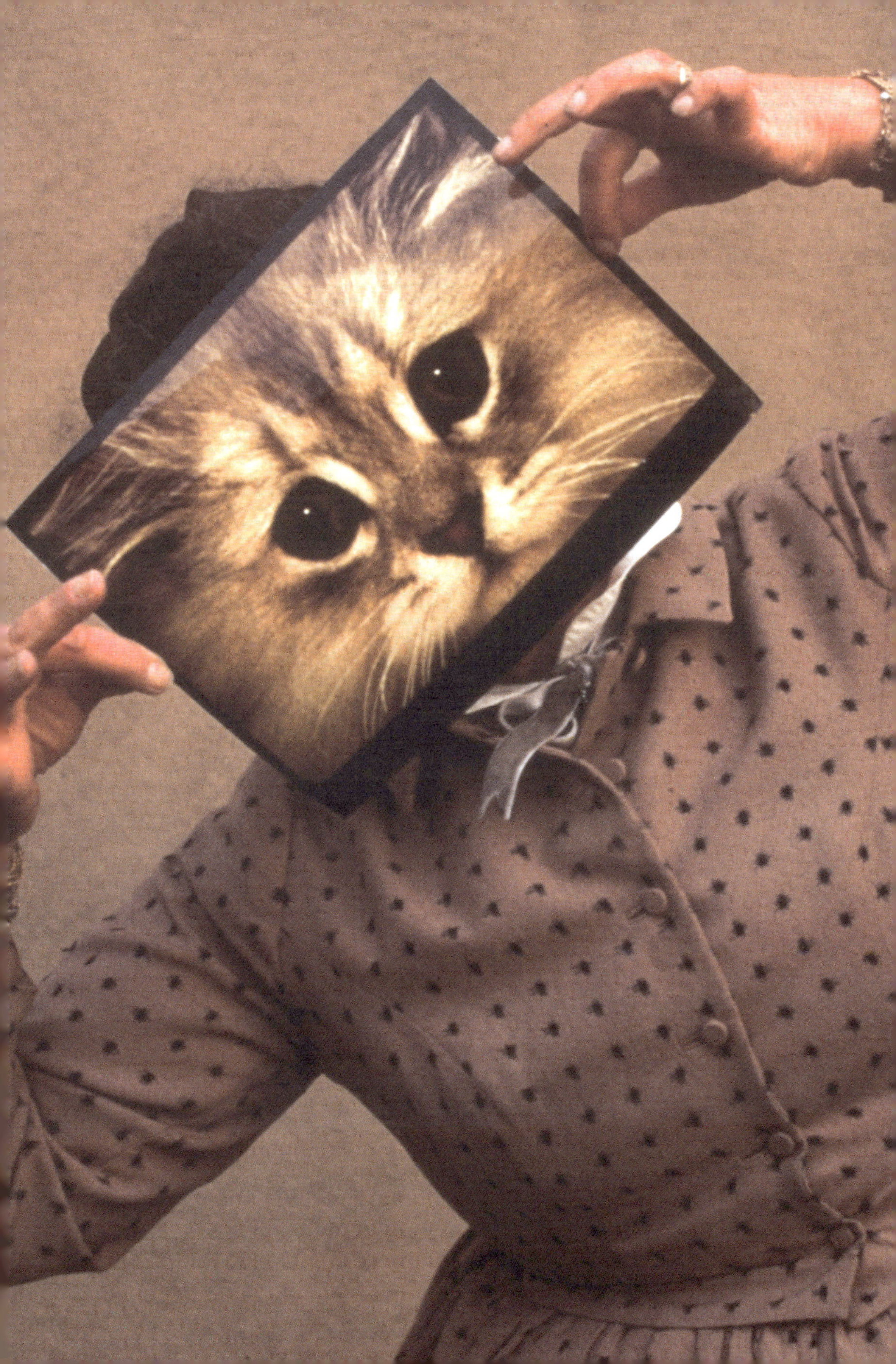

Personalize this book

This is a book about inspiration and ideas and about taking a peek behind the scenes. Because the context in which we operate influences what we talk about, think about and do, it also contains images of encounters, urban landscapes, products, films, exhibitions, etc, etc, photographed by Martí Guixé and Jurgen Bey. We would like to invite you to be the fifth source of inspiration. That is why we included some blank pages for your notes and ideas.

Martí Guixé

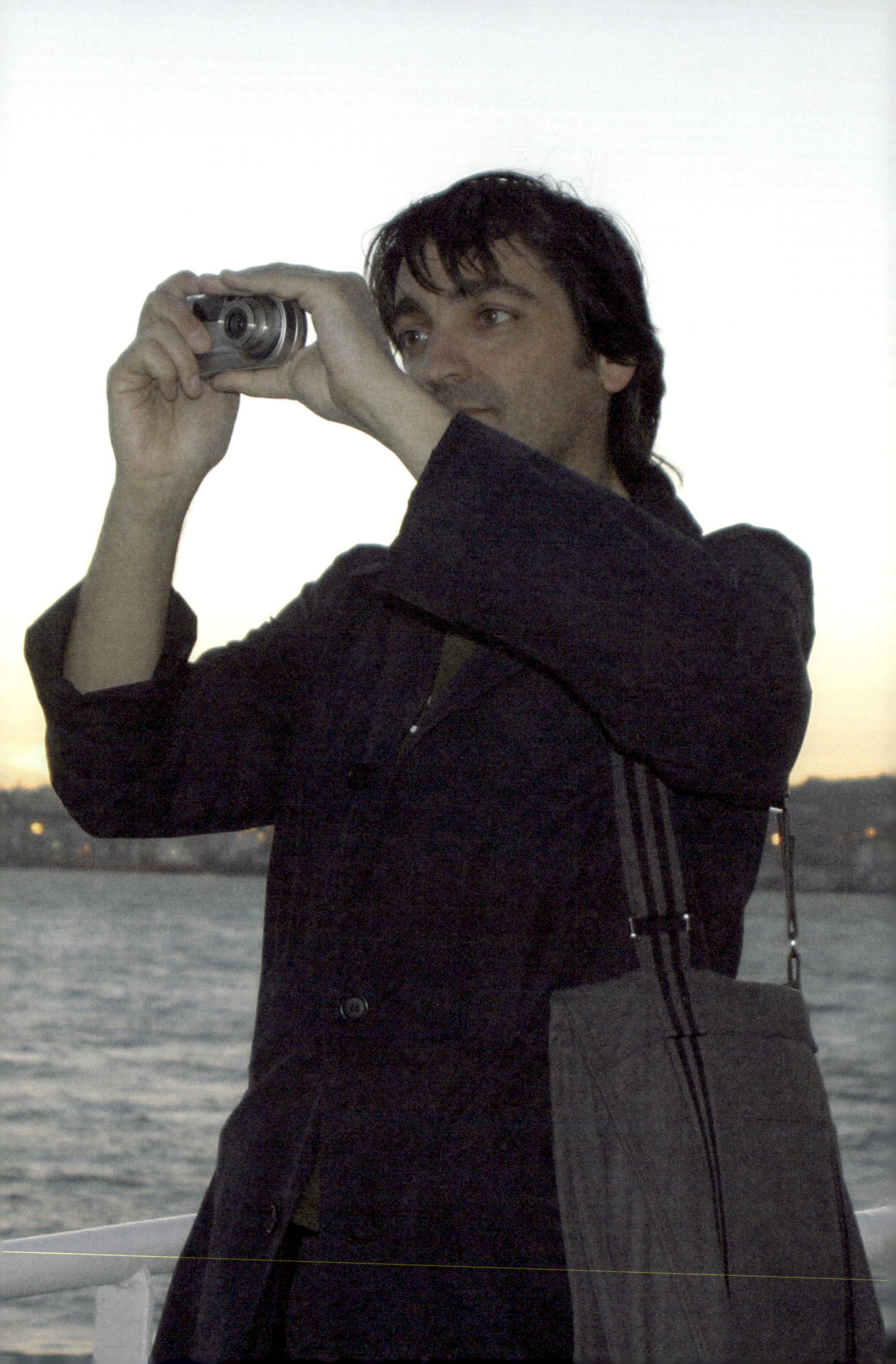

Martí Guixé

Martí Guixé: no objects

The work of Marti Guixé (1964) can be described as 'beyond design'. Guixé is a designer with the mind of an artist, and the 'do-mentality' of a designer. In his search for essential contemporary forms of design, he operates outside current paths and formats. He resoundingly announces his loathing of things, let alone designing them. The latest variant of a chair or other type of furniture he condemns as totally useless. Designers can really no longer afford to ignore all the changes afoot that radically influenced ways that people today live, work and eat. Therefore he himself prefers to concentrate on how things work instead of creating even more objects that prioritise form. As an individual 'global designer', living in Barcelona and Berlin, he prefers to focus on ideas, functions and systems.

Guixé revolutionizes design by working on living matter like food ('the only vital object') and human behavior, which can be transformed and decomposed. He analyses existing situations, rituals and gestures and proposes radically effective solutions with minimal ergonomics. Doing so, he touches areas as anthropology, humour, gastronomy, typography, the human sciences, exact sciences, performance and design. In the end he comes up with simple, inventive and humorous solutions that simplify modern life. Guixé also uses his work to comment on design itself, and the way people use it. All his work is practical as well as a subtle and absurdist, iconoclastic social criticism, full of mischievous in-jokes.

Guixé's career began like those of every other designer with international pretensions. He followed an interior design course at the Elisava School of Design in Barcelona (1983-85) followed by qualifying as an industrial designer at the Scuola Politecnica di Design in Milan (1986-'87), before working for design agencies, and advising the KIDP in Seoul (1994-'96). Since 1997 he has worked independently on projects for, among others, Camper, Authentics, Alessi, Droog Design, Cosmic and Chupa Chups. Besides this, he has presented work in numerous galleries, often with ideas, drawings. objects and installations produced specially for the occasion. He gained renown with immaterial objects such as the index finger ruler tattoo and his 'techno tapas' finger food for today's computer people. Between all the material violence of the design fairs, Guixé's minimalism and subtle humour jumped out. For the same reasons, the work of Guixé was mentioned in the same breath as the Dutch collection Droog Design. His work has grown sharper over the last few years, more serious for those with a good grasp of it, and less material.

Take his 'info shop' proposal for the Majorcan shoe brand Camper, to use the shoebox itself as the basis of the shop design, and to fill the shops with the work and activities of artists and thinkers. Or the plan for Camper, when he proposed to use the near-extinct Majorcan donkey as the brand's symbol. Apart from providing Camper with a sweet cuddly trademark and consumers with a sense of appreciation for their social commitment, it netted a shop full of infotainment and crucial brand reinforcement. Another Camper project included shoeboxes emblazoned with 'If you don't need it don't buy it', a sort of perverted advert that went down a storm. With proposals of this sort, Guixé gets three, four or more birds with one stone. While the brand does exceptionally good business investing a relatively modest budget and supports donkey conservationists, artists and thinkers, Guixé realises a successful and constantly changing store layout plus a campaign, without designing a single new object or generating piles of waste, while pampering spoilt consumers by giving them a sense of sharing a critical attitude.

Guixé is a typical contemporary artist-designer who does not experience the paradoxical position he takes to the world and his profession as a limitation, but as a stimulant. He minutely feels the machinations of our consumer society, our experience economy and our contemporary hedonism.

He is part of it yet at the same time tries to take a critical distance; he is fascinated by it and endeavours to elude it. This starting point pervades all his work. Contemporary man should also relate to today, asserts Guixé; most opinions on things like nature, luxury and freedom are still far too involved in a time that is over, and will not reappear. In a society in which everything – our body, the landscape, our food, money, entertainment, and communication – is subject to the laws of consumerism, concepts like 'nature' and 'natural' are merely obsolete and nostalgic ideas in our imagination. Possession has little to do with luxury if you continuously have to ensure that you don't lose what you possess. And notions about uniqueness and innovation are totally outmoded. Terms like 'open source' systems, thrown up by computer jargon, that develop by sharing knowledge and experience, fit far better into our present, constantly changing time, believes Guixé. 'My primary concern is people and their needs', says Guixé, 'not the objects itself'.

On his website, he gives the example of the formula he developed that, when consistently applied, is guaranteed to 'Mandorla', the image of a total aura around the body derived from Christian iconography. 'Mandorla' is the sort of aura Guixé likes to see – great radiance and enjoyment through physical and mental liberation – an ultimate form of luxury.

$$G/L \left(Magik\left(\frac{Fun \times ikonP}{3} + Funktion\right)\right) = Mandorla$$

Why make life unnecessarily complicated? 'Our habits have changed', says Guixé. 'We no longer sit at the table; we eat while surfing on the Internet. But food has not changed. I'm interested in our habits, in the relationship between the body and our actual environment and the process of feeding ourselves.' Guixé sees countless possibilities for dealing with the familiar, differently. They're there for the taking. You just need to see them and ask the right questions. His proposals and ideas are sometimes so simple that you wonder why you didn't come up with them yourself – if you didn't already. A lolly with a triangular stick so that it doesn't stick when you put it down. A removable tattoo of a subway map you can stick on the palm of your hand. Tape you can stick in your hall or office for a sense of 'greenery' without having to add high-maintenance plants. Pills for cultural acclimatisation or sex appeal, a chair that grows with you and a lamp that recharges using the light of other lamps and that glows for 20 minutes after being switched off so that it never suddenly goes dark. Guixé often doesn't make the ingredients of his designs himself; a simple card with instructions is often sufficient. By suggesting ways of using existing components differently the familiar becomes new and vice versa. And there's money and time to spare.

In fact Guixé is a multidisciplinary global thinker whose outcome has been landed in a context of art and design. His way of thinking corresponds to that of other commentators of the consumer society and the new economy. The most unusual thing about Guixé isn't so much his art and design practice of doing-a-lot-with-a-little, or the fact that he takes a critical attitude to today's overconsumption. What's special about Guixé is that everything he says does and makes feeds into the world he is creating: the Marti Guixé brand. What he wants is part and parcel of what he is. The exdesigner Marti Guixé and his work together form a total concept that is simultaneously appealing, alienating, witty, crazy, intelligent, out of the ordinary and a little irritating. He does this deliberately – is unable to do otherwise – which is why, in the end, he is convincing.

Now that the potential of his ideas is noted worldwide, he is probably the first designer that can live by designing systems and instructions rather than products. That he is also doing relatively well in the art world at the moment is due to the fact that art is assiduously searching for a way out of the isolation of the world of galleries and museums.

Someone like Guixé is popular because is both a contemporary and independent thinker and someone who designs and makes things that have a place in ordinary everyday life. Artistic, critical, practical. As a good artist, Guixé is perfectly happy with this, as long as it works towards his freedom of movement.

Ineke Schwartz

"Hi, I'm Marti, I'm an ex-designer"
an interview with Martí Guixé

Basis for this interview was a number of conversations with Martí Guixé during the workshop 'Beyond consumption' that found place in may 2003 in Lisbon in connection with Experimenta-Design 2003. Two of the answers are of another origin, namely the interview by Brigitte Rambaud that was published in the book 'Martí Guixé 1:1'; these are quoted because Guixé explains there perfectly how possessing objects turned from a blessing into a nuisance, and how he himself tries to avoid products and avoids to design them.

Ineke Schwartz (IS): *You are a designer but you call yourself an ex-designer. What exactly is the reason?*
Martí Guixé (MG): Initially I was not taken seriously. People said I did not make design because my work did not fit the convention what fits a designer. But it also was no art, for it is always in some way commercial. So I'd better design my own category, I thought: that of the ex-designer. Now I am in free space, a very comfortable position.

IS: *For an ex-designer you have a lot to do with the art world. You have interviews with art magazines and exhibitions in galleries. How do you relate to the art world?*
MG: Artists don't want to deal with economy, gallerists do that for them. A video for commercial purposes is not possible in the art world. The art world says I should not collaborate. I accept these conditions, though, and deal with them. The art world follows traditions and conventions that do not fit what people want. Art is a good product, that I just want to consume. The art world should be redesigned.

IS: *You have a love-hate relationship with products. You say all the time you hate them, but then you add 'but I am a designer'. Please explain.*
MG: I am still interested in the function of objects, though I have no thing about possessing them. I believe that during the post-war (1950) the acquisition, possession and representation of objects had a social and moral value, so that with them you purchased happiness and (as with cars) in turn they made you free. Now however the situation is completely opposite, as possession weighs you down and enslaves you to the fear of loss; you lose mobility and time, values in a society of constant change.

My training is as a designer, both interior and industrial design. I now have a contradiction because while I try to not possess objects, considering them unnecessary and even feeling a certain aversion towards them, the only way I have to express my idea is through them. Thus these objects express the absurdity of a culture based on the representation, possession and accumulation of material wealth.

IS: *How do you design without coming up with objects?*
MG: Many of the functions supplied by these objects are irreplaceable. I try to see how these objects might lose their form but continue with their function. This is done using various systems: by assimilation, one product assimilates another, so that one of the two might disappear; by reduction, working with the minimization or dematerialization of these products, making them smaller or invisible; by socialization, so that the product does not need to be purchased or possessed, allowing it be found for free or enabling it to be requested or stolen; by appropriation, so that the function appropriates a space or product and thus is regenerated or becomes necessary; by transmission of the idea, so that the product only transmits information, not being necessary to buy it or even touch it, just know it; or by just ignoring it, considering the product has no value and so you just ignore it.

IS: *How do you make companies accept your proposals?*
MG: It's very easy: as long as companies make profit, they accept everything and you are the king. If not, you are out. More or less it does not matter what you do, really; when they trust you every-

thing is possible. Apart from money it is about image and prestige. Sometimes in a very indirect way, for instance in case of products that don't sell but are published in every magazine and therefore trendy. A lot of products are quite bad but they do sell because there is a lot of money available for representation. Pure bragging. You can work with that idea...

IS: *So you succeed in being a designer without designing products?*
MG: A product is not a physical element but something you can sell, and it must have a name ('If you don't give things a name, they disappear', they say in South Africa, like the Quagga became extinct because he had no name). I did several systems, like the temporary camper shop system. The point is that the systems give you a product, an interior or an object. I can live without designing products, doing instructions, but finally these systems produce a product. I think is more the idea that what I do is more focused in a system than in a shape, and shape or color or material could be anyone. Take the example of the H2O chair. I could say by phone 'make a chair that is so low that you can put books on it, so you regulate the height, do it this and that way' - that's the design of the H2O chair, shape, color and material is then adapted to the local taste - in this case as my client is the gallery H2O, to the taste and parameters of their production - but it doesn't affect the basic concept. Another example is the Temporary Camper shop. Camper asked me to do a shop but I did a system that the people who produce it should interpret, so that my design is the system and the shop is a consequence of this system, but not my design (in some way). This makes it easy to produce, as there are no fixed norms, and it can be adapted (in Milan it was build by architects, in Paris by a company who builds stands) to the construction processes, and the fact that it is different in a different context is not a problem but the interesting thing on it.
A shape is something very local anyway. In a global context it works only if you want to colonize areas with shapes.

IS: *You speak about 'being contemporary' all the time. What are the characteristics of real contemporary design?*
MG: Being really contemporary is very complicated. It is about the freedom to use things for reasons that are not representatative. Using is more important that possessing. It is about the notion that all is insecure: everything changes so much and so fast that nothing is forever, so you have to move, not only physically but also mentally. Being contemporary is about being mobile, adaptable and customizable, so that you can adapt things to your own necessities and your own surroundings. If something has no fixed shape, it can adapt to any shape. It is about reducing - reduce matter, not complexity. Being schematic and impersonal is important, so no overdesign in finishing or in materials and uses, and the more impersonal it is, the more it fits globally. It is also about luxury, not in the sense of representation but in the sense of the intelligence to adapt to situations. 'Luxury' usually means gold or material quality; to me luxury means the possibility not to follow convention and the freedom to have my own system and make my own rituals.

IS: *That way you escape the consumerism that you dislike so much?*
MG: No. Everything is based on the idea that we live in a consumer society and that we are decadent people. You don't really need many things, if you are poor there is little to loose, but it is difficult to escape consumerism. Poor people are seduced by the image of the happy consumer. And everything is a product. If you are sitting in a workshop you are consuming cultural activities. You consume nature by buying special things to enjoy it. Going to Iraq means 20 years more of consumerism. To imagine that you can design an 'ecological' object is nonsense, at best you can try to contaminate less. The best thing to do is to avoid products.

IS: *Can an ex-designer change the world?*
MG: Of course I want to change society. My work is full of statements and things that try

to change the attitude of people. Though there is no intention to annul attitudes or force people to change. The idea is to propose intelligent alternatives by means of small mechanisms, sometimes in the form of information, sometimes as objects, sometimes as a change in the attitude objects are viewed with. I do not believe there is a perfect or ideal attitude. But society has a kind of delay, a kind of codified thing that makes that people don't realize that we live in two different realities now: reality and perception. I try to make distortions in everyday life, so that people realize that subjective reality is standard. If you want to change society, it takes time, but in contemporary society that should not be the case. You should be able to buy a kit for the purpose.

Selected works

Functional Tattoos, 1997

The idea was to return tattoos to the functionality they had before they were transformed into fashion. I configured several removable tattoos for contemporary functions. The Designer tattoo allows you to measure at any time. The business tattoos are small devices to carry or deal with information. The tourist tattoo consists of a subway map, which you tattoo on your hand (removable). This way you always have your map to hand.

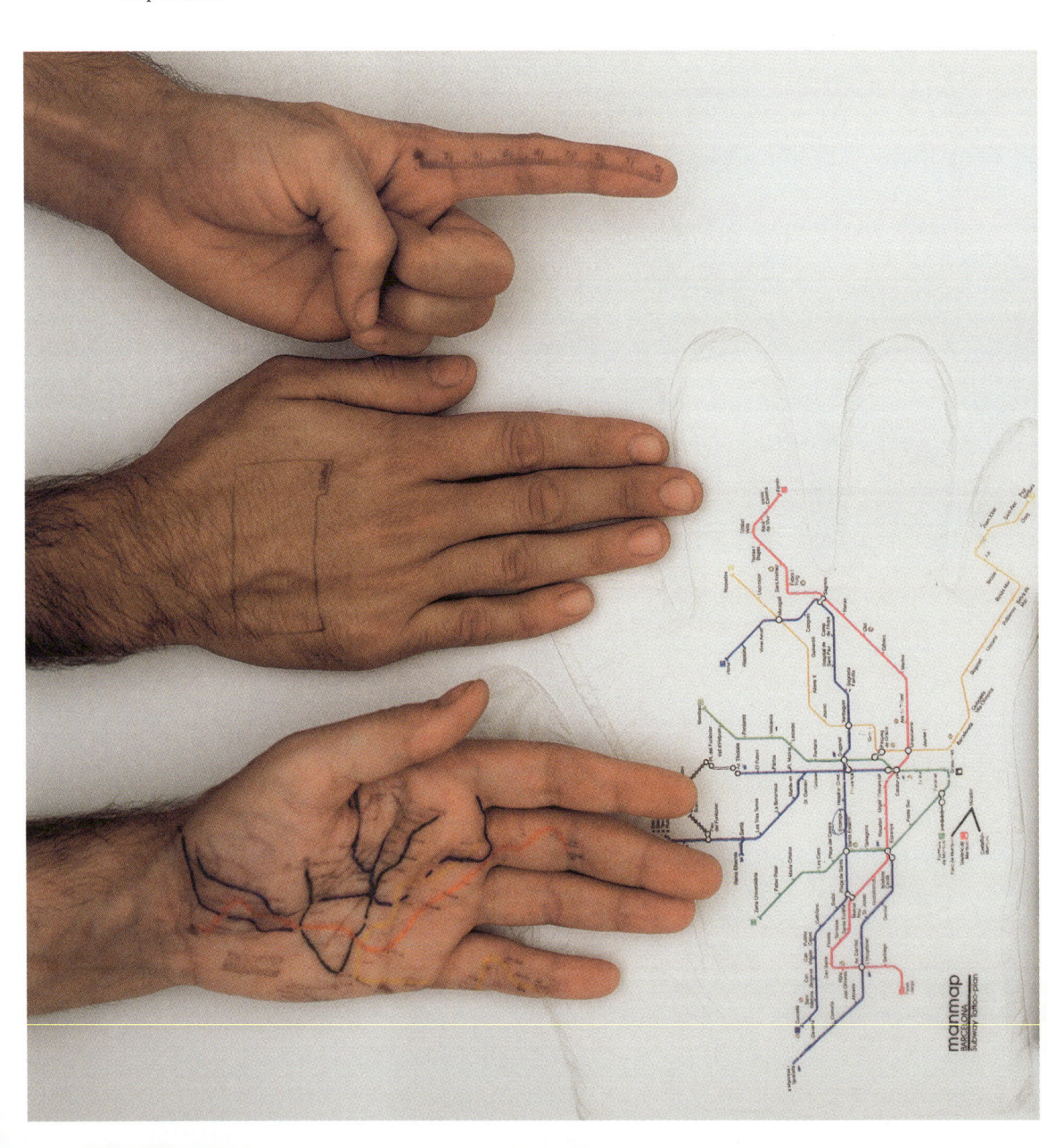

Sponsored Food, 1997

The Ck Potato Omelette, Fuji Onion Omelette & IBM Bean. I never thought of Sponsored Food as a system for poor people or the Third World. I made the concept of Sponsored Food for my artist friends, who need to work in bad jobs to make enough money to survive, which has had great deal of negative influence on their artistic work. The idea of creating a network of sponsored food restaurants would allow people to be free from the social behavior that comes from the necessity of surviving (competitiveness, work, supporting the family).

To eat for free would unavoidably provoke unforeseeable reactions and social transformations. With Sponsored Food there are two parallel ideas evident: the sense of nature at the beginning of humanity and contemporary capitalism.

137 ARE NOW MAJOR-CAN.

CAMPER

Camper
Top left: Camper London (Old Bond street), 2003
Down left: Camper Frankfurt (Goethestraße), 2002
Right: Camper Milano (Via Monte Napoleone), 1999

Football tape, 2000
Tape with football pattern, once rolled it up it transforms into a football.
Private edition.

I-cakes, 2001

The pie chart indicates the quantity of the cake ingredients in %. Decoration becomes information. Prototypes.

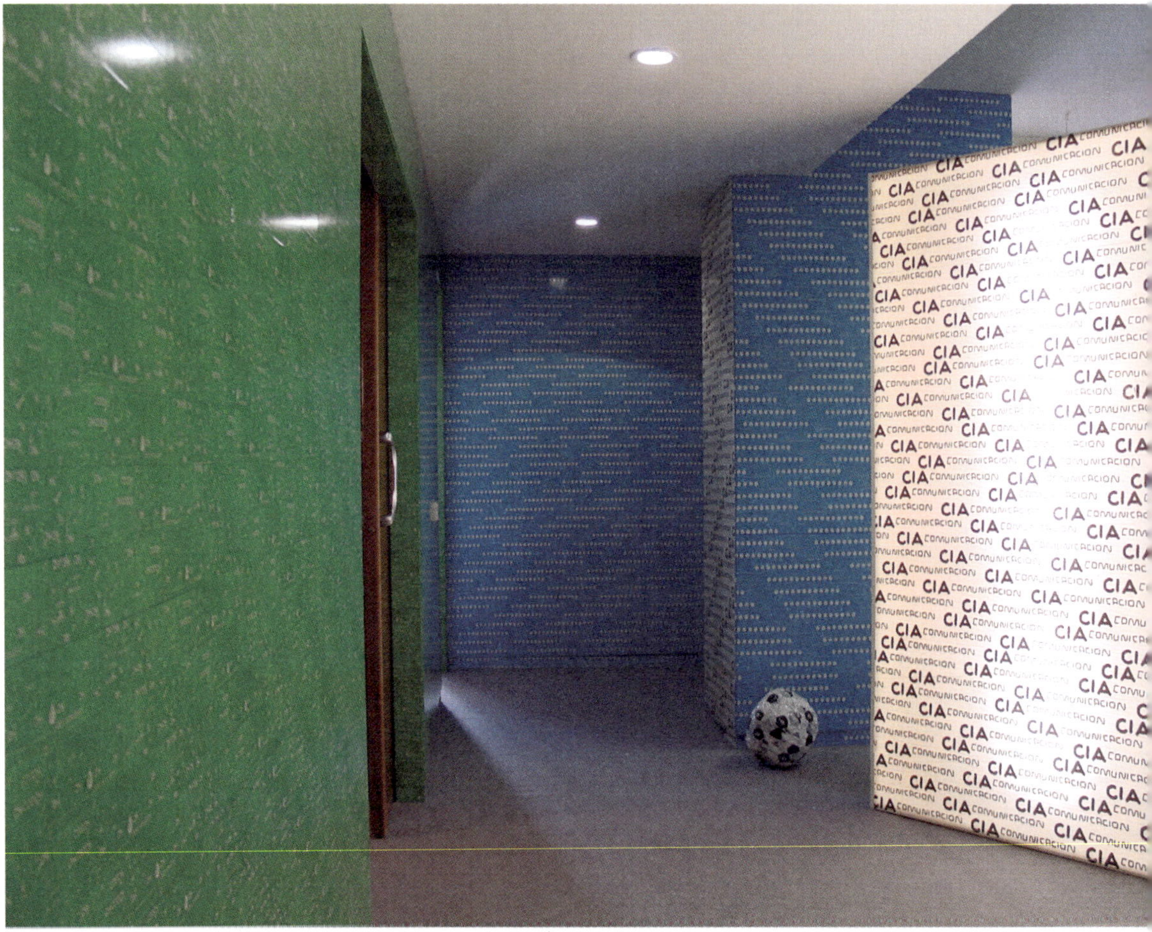
CIA COMUNICACION

CIACOMUNICACIÓN

Is a graphic communication agency in Barcelona. Joan Armengol, a friend of mine, who is one of the founders, requested that I do some sort of installation in the entrance way. I proposed a 'Taping' action, where all the walls of the agency were covered in adhesive tape. Guest tape, relax tape, plant emulator 1.0 tape and others refer directly to 'CIACOMUNICACIÓN' and its concept of teamwork.

'CIACOMUNICACIÓN' Barcelona/Installation, 2002

Martí Guixé

Hibye card, 2001

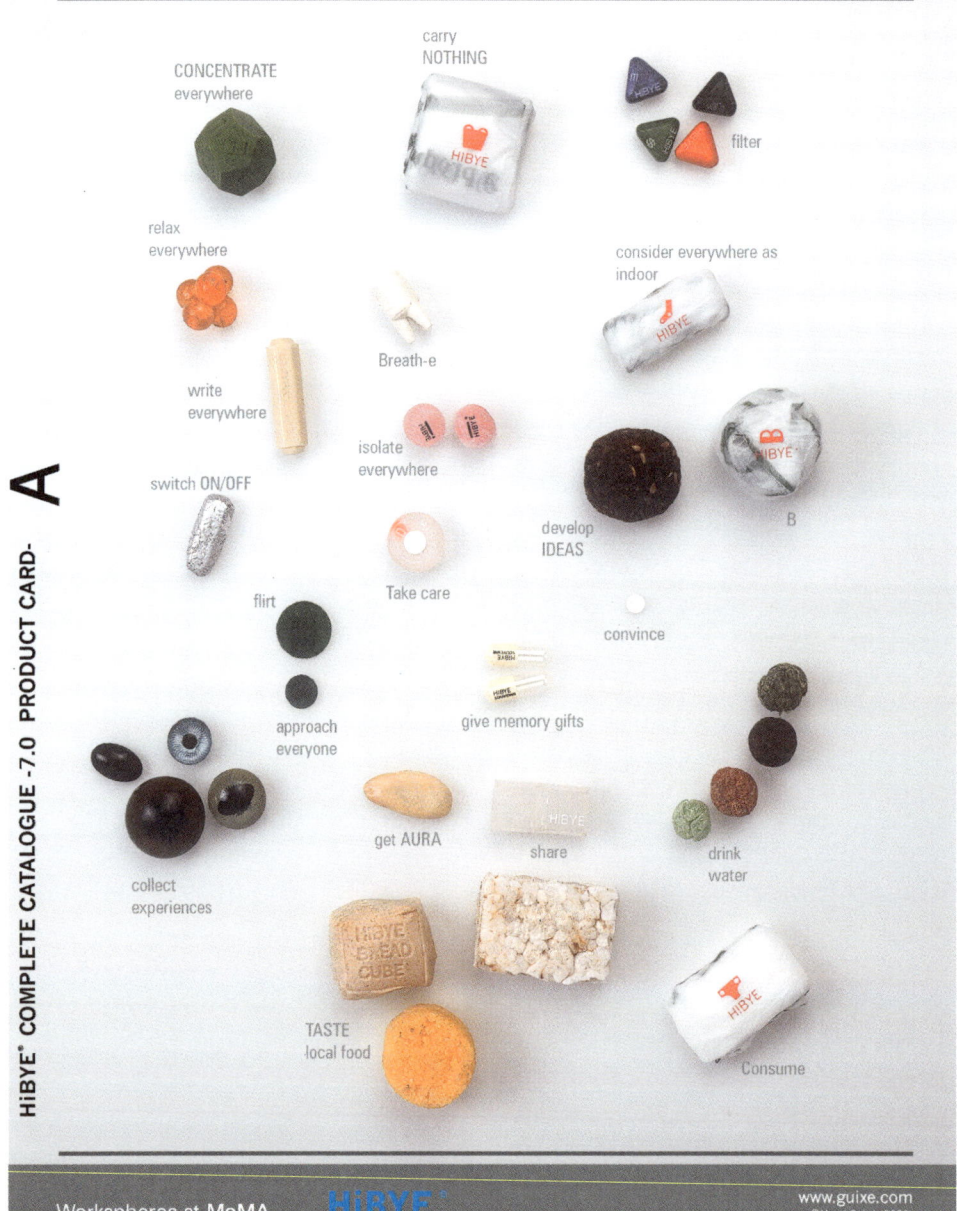

Hibye. Nomadic Worksphere seeds. Basic units for nomadic working (in generic spaces such airports, airplanes, trains, hi-ways and MoMA) worldwide. *Project.*

117 BRIGHT MINDS, BEAUTIFUL IDEAS

HiBYE® 7.0
COMPLETE PRODUCT CATALOGUE - CARD -

Nomadic Worksphere Seeds
Basic units for nomadic working (in generic spaces such airports, airplanes, trains, hi-ways and MoMA) world wide.

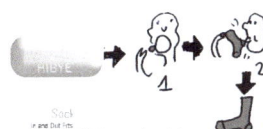

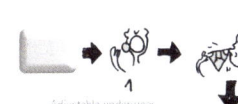

Concentration
CONCENTRATION IS EVERYWHERE
Office is everywhere you are. Non active hard pill to play with and get concentrated for work. You can also play with it in your hand.

Chill out
RELAX IS EVERYWHERE
Non active soft unit to play with in your mouth and to get relaxed.

Breath Set up / Pocket Window
Nomadic cultures are based on Oral communication. Same as the nomadic worker's culture. It is a edible ampule to get fresh breath. Pocket window effect. Fresh Sarass air is inside, you can be outside without leaving generic closed spaces. For regenerating yourself.

Orality Writing
WRITE ALL OVER
A unit that allows writing all over. You can eat it too. You can use any surface and wipe it out easily.

OFC
APPROACH EVERYONE EVERYWHERE
A good nomadic worker takes information from the rest, speaking with people everywhere is a way of acquiring fresh useful 1st hand information. Information is for nomadic work matter. Ope-patch, you take it to the mouth and then you stick it on any part of your body. Saliva is used to activate the sticker substance.

Sex appeal
Perfume patch, you take it to the mouth and then you stick it on any part of your body. Saliva is used to activate the sticker substance. Refers to the private image, defines the personal relation between yourself and the rest of the people.

Sensory Reductors
ISOLATE YOURSELF EVERYWHERE
Edible 'prepear', you take it to the mouth and then it becomes soft. You introduce it in your ears or nose or pull it on your eyes. Saliva is used to get different kind of softness. After using you can eat them. A way of disconnecting yourself from hearing or smelling or seeing the surrounding.

Dr. YOU
Portable doctor.
It is a multi-tablet (cocktail) that provides you all you need to get healthy in any kind of light illness. 100% natural !

GO Crazy switch
In work situations you need a kind of reaction to refresh your mind. This unit provides you with strong sensation. It is made of Aluminum that reacts with your teeth implants. Non edible.

Food
BASIC POPS
Snacks made of basic nutrient elements from the world: wheat, corn, rice.
1 Corn nugget
2 Rice Ball
3 Bread

Culture Bridge
FEEL COMFORTABLE EVERYWHERE
A unit that provides you with specific regional or continental natural flavors combined with digestive spices that you can put over the generic food of airplanes and generic restaurants.
1 American spices
2 Asian spices
3 European spices
4 African spices

Drinks
POCKET DRINKS
Get water in generic spaces. This unit allows you to make tea or coffee with a glass of water. Attention! You put the unit in your mouth and then you drink. You make the tea for the coffee in your mouth!
1 Green tea
2 Mint tea
3 Bio tea
4 Coffee

Thrill sweets
COLLECT EXPERIENCES
Experiences are necessary for life. Work travelers have no experiences in generic spaces. Full flavored candies in the shape of toys eyes (for example teddy bears) to combat dullness in generic spaces.
1 Teddy bear eye
2 Teddy dog eye
3 Doll eye
4 Teddy Tiger eye

Communicator
Share!
Alcohol unit as a usemaker for communication. Communication is a tool for nomadic work → information.

Idea Ball
SPREAD IDEAS
Masanobu Fukuoka is a Japanese man that invented years ago a very funny and rigorous functional system to reforest planet earth. It consists in performing seed balls with earth. You throw it away in the landscape and they are there waiting for the ideal conditions to germinate.
Idea ball is an energy amplifier to eat. Dry fruits with coffee glue pastry mixture. An energetic ball to germinate situations on the way.

AURA comes
GET AURA
The only reason for most people personally is to feel and to contrast auras. The unit is an Almond (Mandorla) unit. Mandorla is the name Marti Guixé gives to the aura in his formula. Aura comes is the real time performance effect.

Sock
In and Out Fits
Basic needs are fulfilled through units that you dissolve in your mouth and you get the object. Made of organic material, they adjust to your body when you put them on. Should be single use only. Designed are only "non lock" elements, the look clothes should change because of fashion or situations or cultural reasons.

Breast Cover
IN and Out Fits

Adjustable underwear
IN and Out Fits

Peripheral
CARRY NOTHING
Don't transport matter, transport information, when there is no possibility, here is the bag. Could be sponsored. It works like the underwear units and it is multi functional.

Patch system that allows to perform better real time communication by establishing (building) designed look areas in your face.
1 Business
2 Private
3 Traveling

Talking Object

Souvenir
Take a small object of the place where you experienced a good story and put this piece into the capsule. Once you want to activate the memory take capsule, put it in your mouth and start telling the story, the unit dissolvers into your mouth while you explain the story. Once finished you take the small object and give it to the audience.

HiBYE® COMPLETE CATALOGUE -7.0 PRODUCT CARD- B

Workspheres at MoMA   HiBYE®   www.guixe.com
©Martí Guixé (2000)

Cacao dune, 2001
Natural object for the home or office interior

Remake
This picture is taken of a remake of the original cacao dune made by Martí Guixé. We bought 1 kilo of cacao at the nearest by food store. We went outside with a sheet of white paper (A0) and a digital camera. We threw the cacao without any specific feeling on the white paper, trying to create a dune as in the 1:1 catalogue from Marti Guixé. Our cacao had sort of rock pieces and we decided not to buy another pack. We made a picture of it and went to the computer. On the screen it looks like an island instead of a dune. We worked a bit with photoshop as well. Try to do this at home. We do not know what Martí thinks of this.

Looking back in the catalogue '1:1' we suddenly notice a very tiny little glimmering edge on the left side of the cacao dune. We think Martí used glue to throw the cacao on and then he blew the cacao dust away.

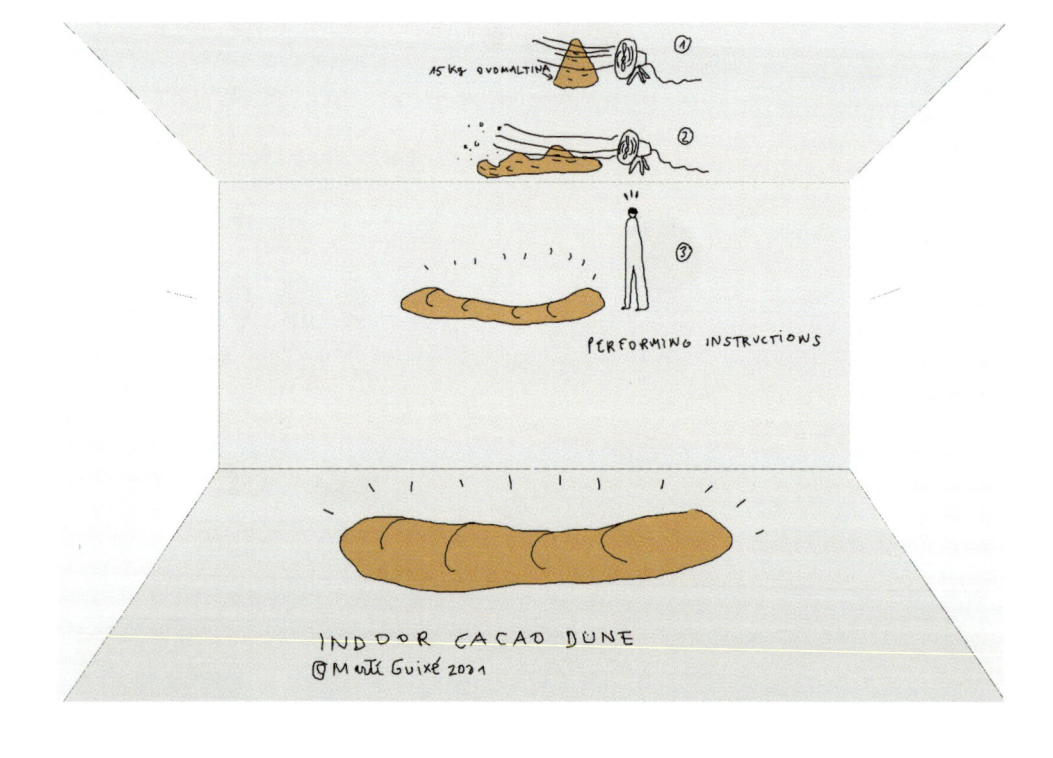

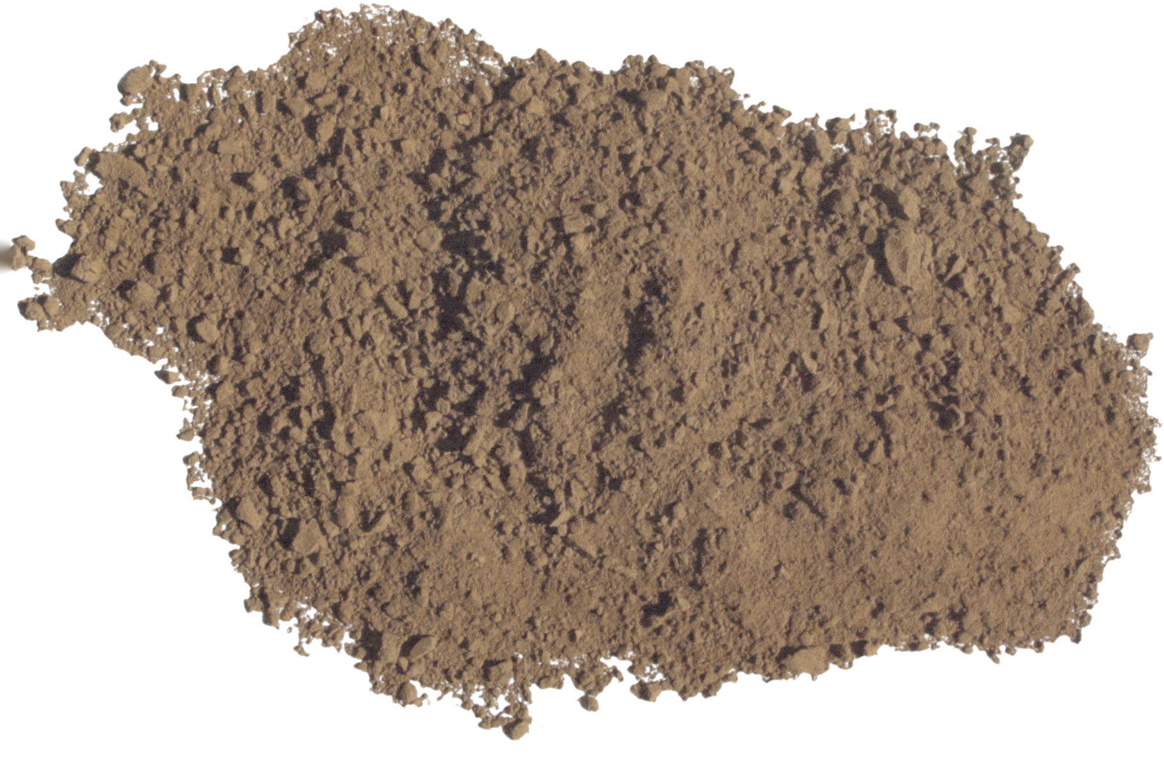

Gin Tonic puddle, 2000
Natural object for the home or office interior

Remake
The 'Gin Tonic puddle' is a peculiar thing. Mixed fluids mend to be consumed in a glass. This puddle is not for mouth consumption. It is for nose consumption. We went to a liquor shop and asked for the best Gin (many good ones, the man says) and the best tonic (just one with the yellow sticker). Back in the Studio we poured the Gin in a water bottle and the water in the gin bottle (why spill the gin for the picture?. Nobody will smell it in the book!). On the picture; the hands of our intern Mana pours the water and the Tonic on top of the small meeting table (Ed was sitting on his knees on the table making the picture). Afterwards we had a nice Gin Tonic drink. And then we decided to make the puddle again with Gin and Tonic.

Oranienbaum Lollipop, 1999

An orange candy lollipop containing a single seed. A way to activate sporadic and spontaneous reforestation just by spitting out the seed once the candy is finished. Prototype.

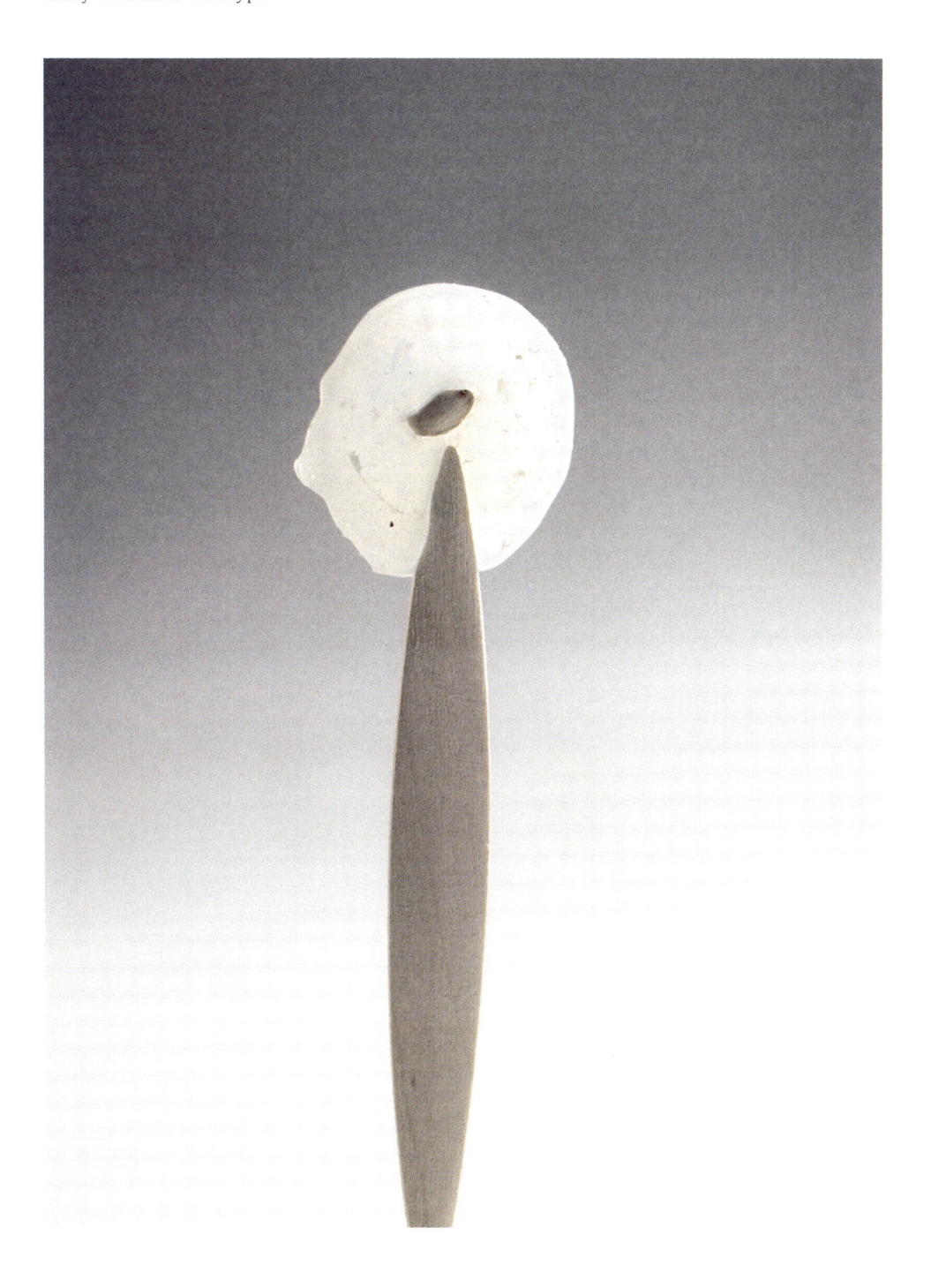

Plato conbinado, 2001
System to combine food ingredients through genetic theories. The four variables are sea, land, carbohydrates and vegetables, which are combined mathematically. Concept.

AABB	AABb	AaBB	AaBb
AABb	AAbb	AaBb	Aabb
AaBB	AaBb	aaBB	aaBb
AaBb	Aabb	aaBb	aabb

H2O ring, 2003

'Non visible ring' is a silver ring painted in a skin tone. It is a ring to seal verbal, unwritten contracts. Produced by 'Galeria H2O' in an edition of 10 signed and numbered units.

MTKS-3

The Meta-territorial Kitchen Sytem-3
– A year 2003 Contemporary kitchen –

The Meta Territorial Kitchen System-3 was developed by Martí Guixé especially for the 'Bright Minds, Beautiful Ideas' project, and was used as a starting point for the workshop.

1
The concept: The kitchen as interface
The kitchen is not an atelier, nor a laboratory, but an interface where we deal with resources that we can open or not, install, uninstall, execute, etc. The basis is an open operative platform

2
Open source code system
All the people, and not only professionals, have the possibility to design new tools based in the operative system

3
The object: A console
Status = Contemporary
X/3 reduced
Luxus, based in the capacity to question the convention
To use not to posses
Informal, not provisional
Schematic
Impersonal/customisable

4
The construction: de-professionalization of the construction, configuration and customisation.

5
Food: the meta-territorial cuisine

6
Homage-reference to Eames kitchen debate.

What's NEW?
- You can buy it piece by piece
- You don't need a previous planning before installation
- Can grow and change
- Adapts to exceptional situations:
  Cooking for a lot of people;
  Change of cooking room;
  Picnic, outdoor in general;
  Special cooking actions (marmalade making for example)
- Allows you give components as a present
- Total mobility from the elements to adapt the composition to the individual personal style
- Allows storage of hardware (like sink, tap, stove) when not used
- Allows interchanging elements with friends or neighbours in some situations or for special occasions
- You can cook any type of food, of any culture, depending in the components you collect and in the way you configure them and you use them.
- Allows expanding the system with new components and new technologies without changing everything
- Allows mixing elements that conventional kitchen doesn't allow, because space reasons, and ideology reasons
- Allows to you to create your own components: Open source.

Martí Guixé
2003

125 BRIGHT MINDS, BEAUTIFUL IDEAS

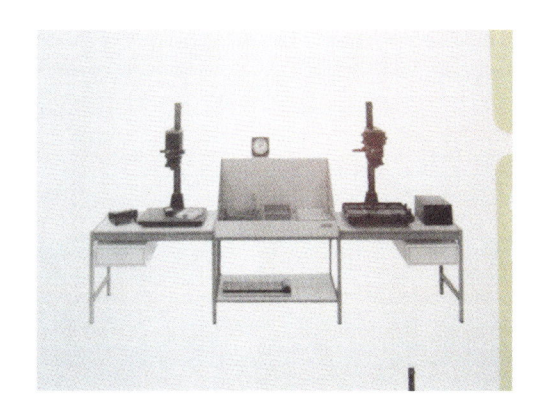

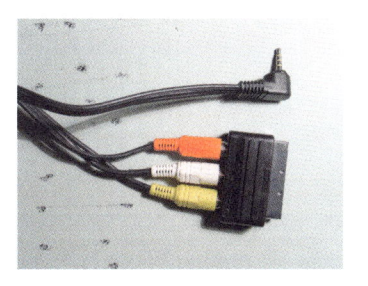

126 BRIGHT MINDS, BEAUTIFUL IDEAS

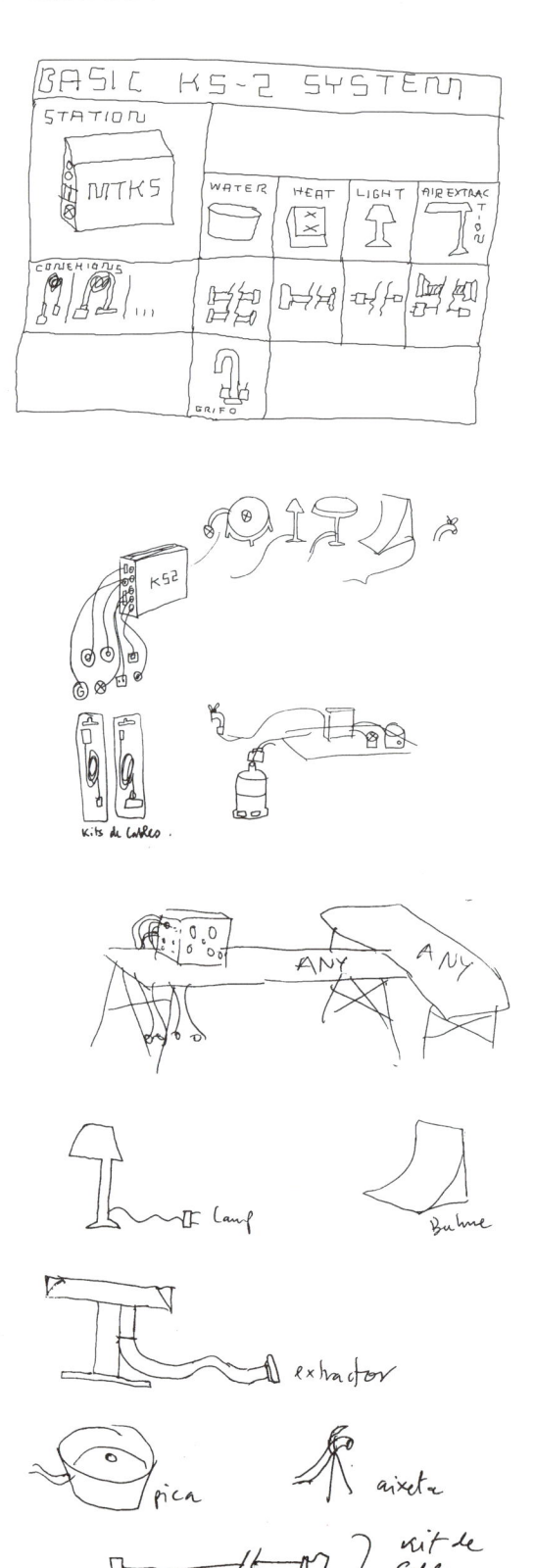

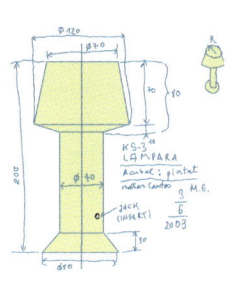

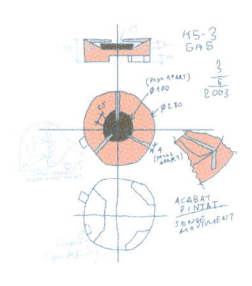

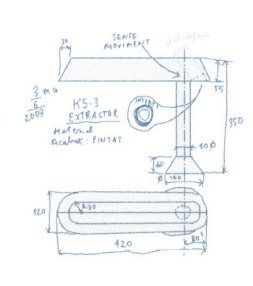

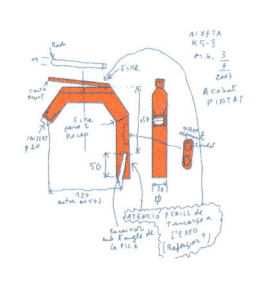

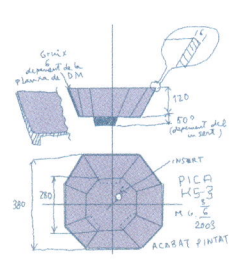

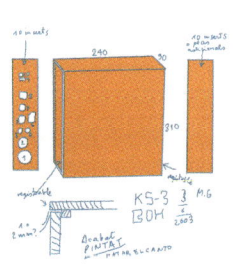

127 BRIGHT MINDS, BEAUTIFUL IDEAS

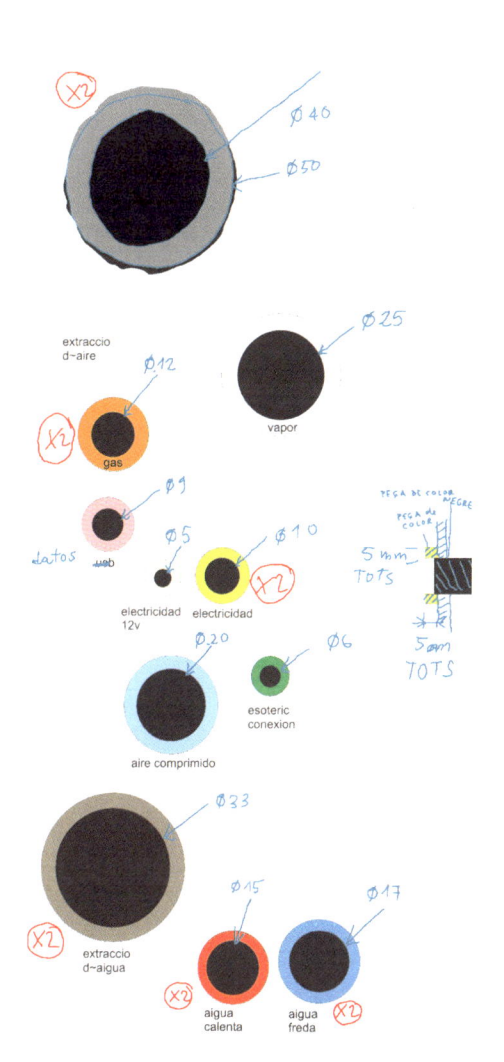

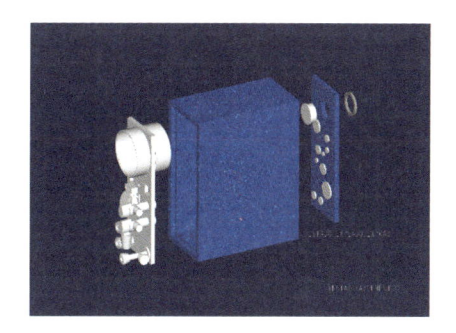

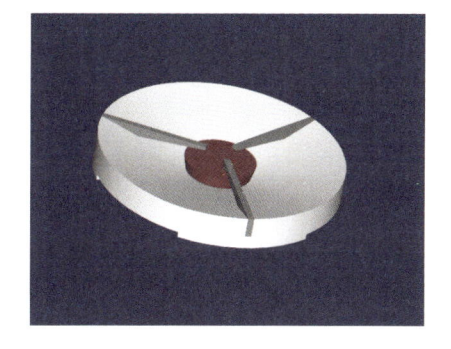

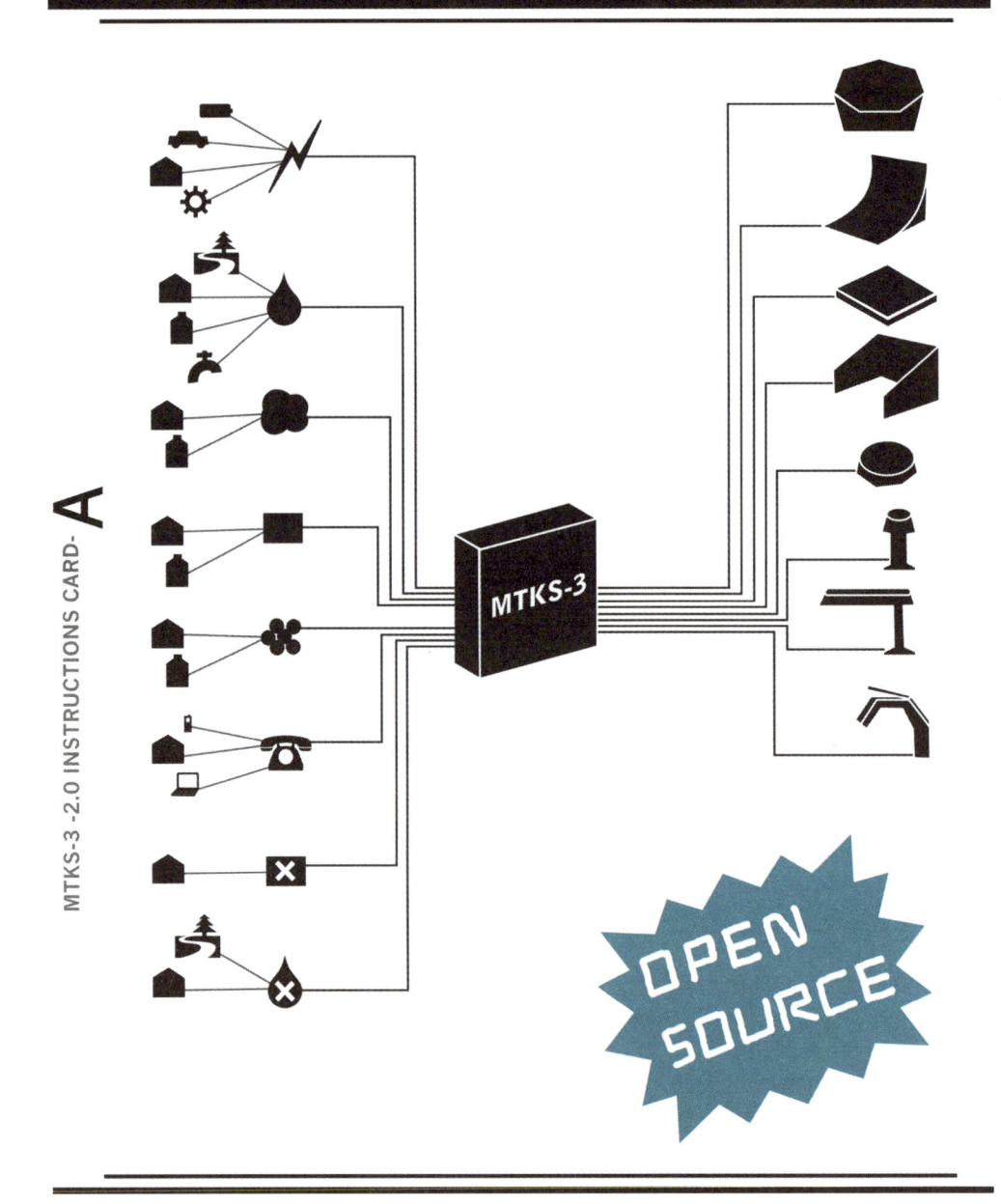

MTKS-3   2.0
Meta Territorial Kitchen System - 3

MTKS-3 -2.0 INSTRUCTIONS CARD- A

OPEN SOURCE

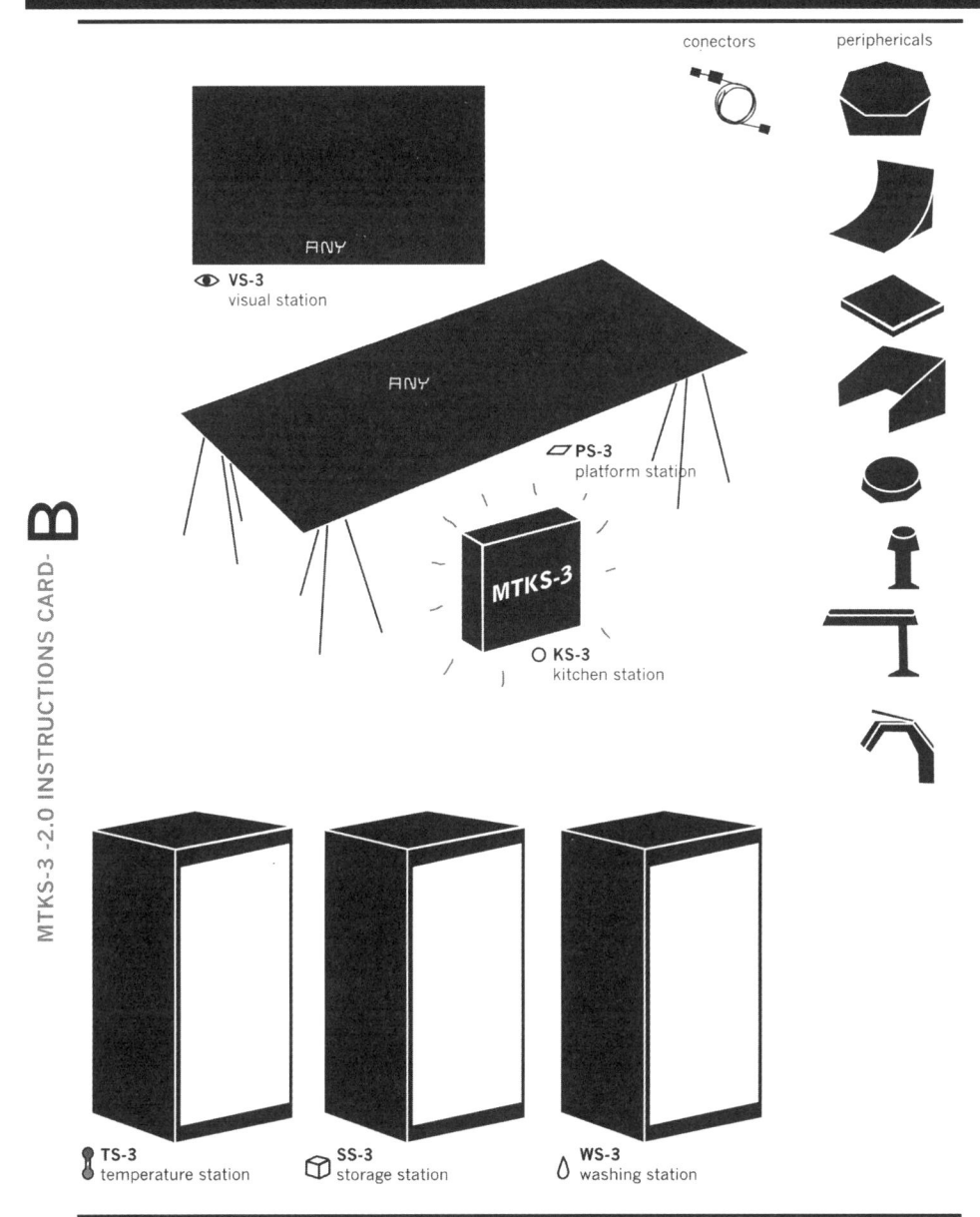

MTKS-3   2.0
Meta Territorial Kitchen System - 3

conectors   periphericals

◉ **VS-3**
visual station

⊿ **PS-3**
platform station

○ **KS-3**
kitchen station

MTKS-3 -2.0 INSTRUCTIONS CARD- B

🌡 **TS-3**
temperature station

⌂ **SS-3**
storage station

◊ **WS-3**
washing station

MTKS-3
The Meta-territorial Kitchen Sytem-3
– A year 2003 Contemporary kitchen –

Martí Guixé, 2003

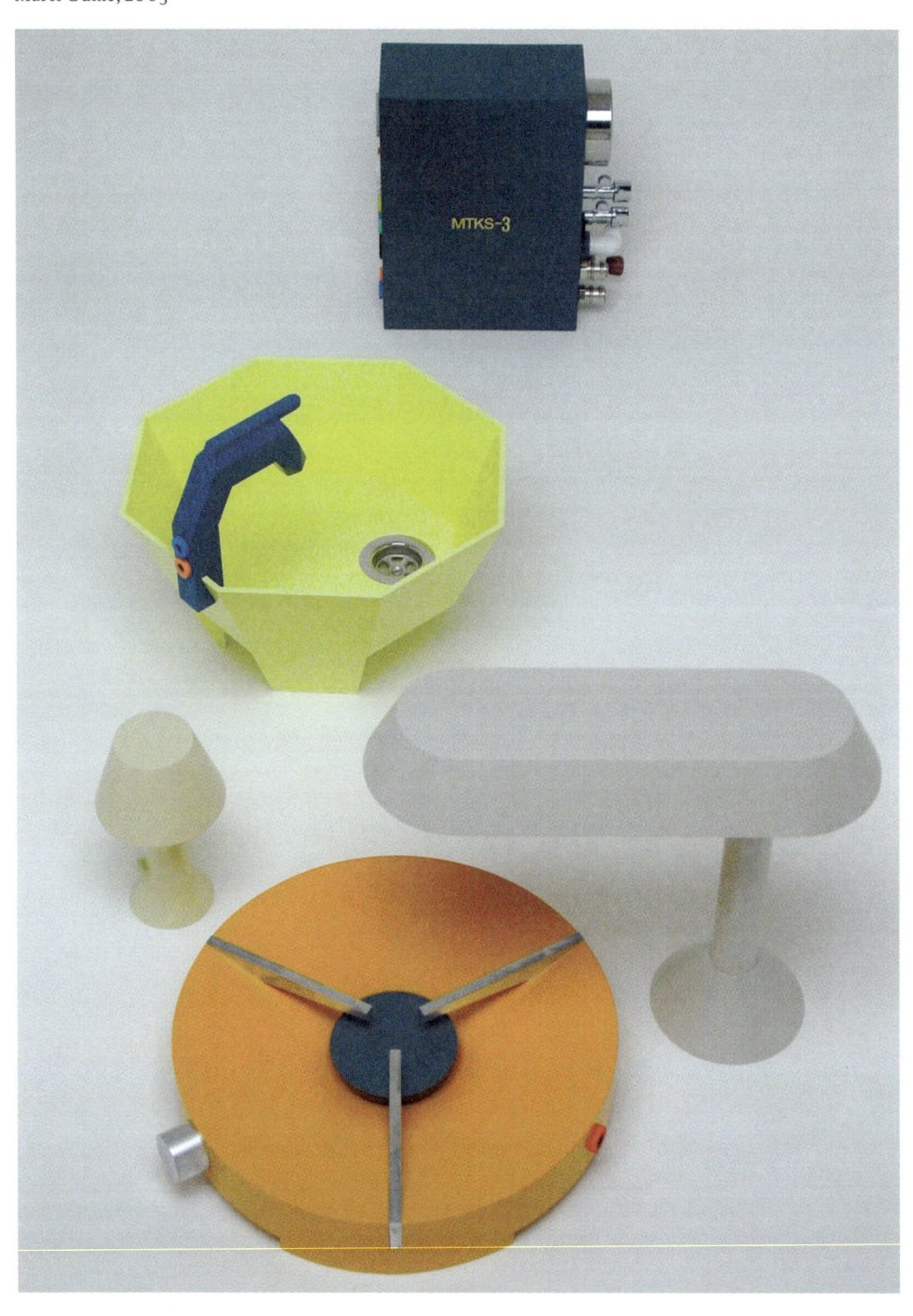

Khrushchev – Nixon
'The Moscow Kitchen debate', 1959

'The Moscow Kitchen debate' is included in this book because it was the motive on which Martí Guixé based his workshop and his Meta-territorial kitchen System-3.

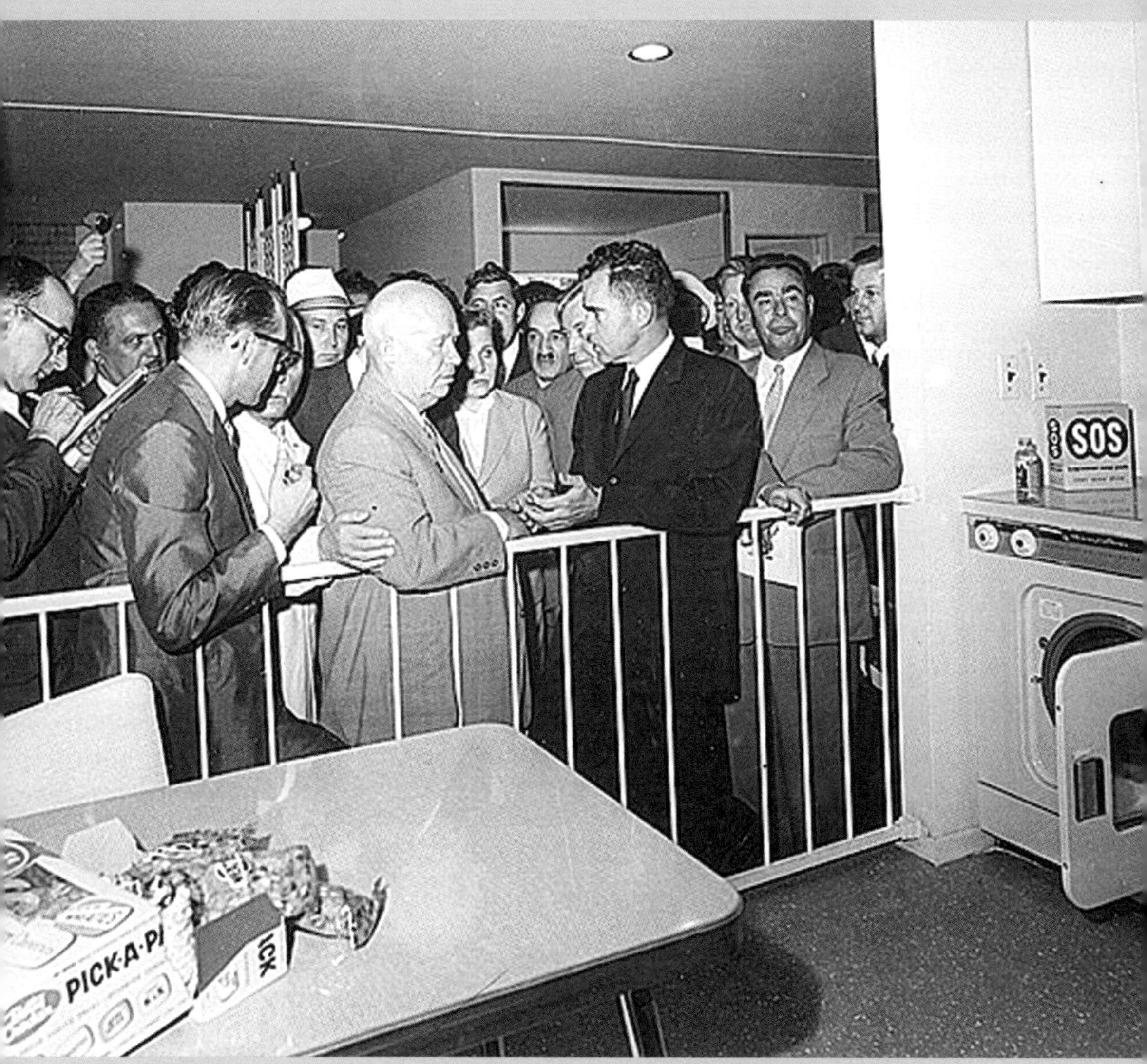
SOS
PICK·A·P
ICK

Khrushchev – Nixon, 'The Moscow Kitchen debate', 1959

On July 24th, 1959, Vice President Richard Nixon and Soviet Premier Nikita Khrushchev held a public discussion at the American National Exhibit in Moscow comparing the technologies of the two powers. In the debate they discussed household items such as color televisions and in the process reviewed differences in ideology and the quality of life in both countries for the average citizen. This edited transcript appeared the following day in The New York Times.

Khrushchev – Nixon
July 24th, 1959

Following is an account of the informal exchanges in Moscow between Vice President Richard M. Nixon and Premier Nikita S. Khrushchev.

Khrushchev: "We want to live in peace and friendship with Americans because we are the two most powerful countries and if we live in friendship then other countries will also live in friendship. But if there is a country that is too war-minded we could pull its ears a little and say: Don't you dare; fighting is not allowed now; this is a period of atomic armament; some foolish one could start a war and then even a wise one couldn't finish the war. Therefore, we are governed by this idea in our policy – internal and foreign. How long has America existed? Three hundred years?"

Nixon: "One hundred and fifty years."

Khrushchev: "One hundred and fifty years? Well then we will say America has been in existence for 150 years and this is the level she has reached. We have existed not quite 42 years and in another seven years we will be on the same level as America. When we catch you up, in passing you by, we will wave to you. Then if you wish we can stop and say: Please follow up. Plainly speaking, if you want capitalism you can live that way. That is your own affair and doesn't concern us. We can still feel sorry for you but since you don't understand us – live as you do understand.

"We are all glad to be here at the exhibition with Vice President Nixon. I personally, and on behalf of my colleagues, express my thanks for the president's message. I have not as yet read it but I know beforehand that it contains good wishes. I think you will be satisfied with your visit and if I cannot go on without saying it – if you would not take such a decision [proclamation by the United States Government of Captive Nations Week, a week of prayer for peoples enslaved by the Soviet Union] which has not been thought out thoroughly, as was approved by Congress, your trip would be excellent. But you have churned the water yourselves – why this was necessary God only knows.

"What happened? What black cat crossed your path and confused you? But that is your affair, we do not interfere with your problems. [Wrapping his arms about a Soviet workman] Does this man look like a slave laborer? [Waving at others] With men with such spirit how can we lose?"

Nixon: [pointing to American workmen] "With men like that we are strong. But these men, Soviet and American, work together well for peace, even as they have worked together in building this exhibition. This is the way it should be. Your remarks are in the tradition of what we have come to expect – sweeping and extemporaneous. Later on we will both have an opportunity to speak and consequently I will not comment on the various points that you raised, except to say this – this color television is one of the most advanced developments in communication that we have.

"I can only say that if this competition in which you plan to outstrip us is to do the best for both of our peoples and for peoples everywhere, there must be a free exchange of ideas. After all, you don't know everything'"

Khrushchev: "If I don't know everything you don't know anything about communism except fear of it."

Nixon: "There are some instances where you may be ahead of us, for example in the development of the thrust of your rockets for the investigation of outer space; there may be some instances in which we are ahead of you – in color television, for instance."

Khrushchev: "No, we are up with you on this, too. We have bested you in one technique and also in the other."

Nixon: "You see, you never concede anything."

Khrushchev: "I do not give up."

Nixon: "Wait till you see the picture. Let's have far more communication and exchange in this very area that we speak of. We should hear you more on our televisions. You should hear us more on yours."

Khrushchev: "That's a good idea. Let's do it like this. You appear before our people.
We will appear before your people. People will see and appreciate this."

Nixon: "There is not a day in the United States when we cannot read what you say.
When Kozlov was speaking in California about peace, you were talking here in somewhat different terms. This was reported extensively in the American press. Never make a statement here if you don't want it to be read in the United States. I can promise you every word you say will be translated into English."

Khrushchev: "I doubt it. I want you to give your word that this speech of mine will be heard by the American people."

Nixon [shaking hands on it]: "By the same token, everything I say will be translated and heard all over the Soviet Union?"

Khrushchev: "That's agreed."

Nixon: "You must not be afraid of ideas."

Khrushchev: "We are telling you not to be afraid of ideas. We have no reason to be afraid. We have already broken free from such a situation."

Nixon: "Well, then, let's have more exchange of them. We are all agreed on that.
All right? All right?"

Khrushchev: "Fine. [Aside] Agree to what? All right, I am in agreement. But I want to stress what I am in agreement with. I know that I am dealing with a very good lawyer.... You are a lawyer for capitalism and I am a lawyer for communism. Let's compare."

Nixon: "The way you dominate the conversation you would make a good lawyer yourself. If you were in the United States Senate you would be accused of filibustering." [Halting Khrushchev at model kitchen in model house]: "You had a very nice house in your exhibition in New York. My wife and I saw and enjoyed it very much. I want to show you this kitchen. It is like those of our houses in California."

Khrushchev: [after Nixon called attention to a built-in panel-controlled washing machine]: "We have such things."

Nixon: "This is the newest model. This is the kind which is built in thousands of units for direct installation in the houses." He added that Americans were interested in making life easier for their women.

Mr. Khrushchev remarked that in the Soviet Union, they did not have "the capitalist attitude toward women."

Nixon: "I think that this attitude toward women is universal. What we want to do is make easier the life of our housewives."

He explained that the house could be built for $14,000 and that most veterans had bought houses for between $10,000 and $15,000.

Nixon: "Let me give you an example you can appreciate. Our steelworkers, as you know, are on strike. But any steelworker could buy this house. They earn $3 an hour. This house costs about $100 a month to buy on a contract running 25 to 30 years."

Khrushchev: "We have steel workers and we have peasants who also can afford to spend $14,000 for a house."

He said American houses were built to last only 20 years, so builders could sell new houses at the end of that period

"We build firmly. We build for our children and grandchildren."

Mr. Nixon said he thought American houses would last more than 20 years, but even so, after 20 years many Americans want a new home or a new kitchen, which would be obsolete then. The American system is designed to take advantage of new inventions and new techniques, he said.

Khrushchev: "This theory does not hold water."

He said some things never got out of date – furniture and furnishings, perhaps, but not houses. He said he did not think houses. He said he did not think that what Americans had written about their houses was all strictly accurate.

Nixon [pointing to television screen]: "We can see here what is happening in other parts of the home."

Khrushchev: "This is probably always out of order."
Nixon: "Da [yes]"

Khrushchev: "Don't you have a machine that puts food into the mouth and pushes it down? Many things you've shown us are interesting but they are not needed in life. They have no useful purpose. They are merely gadgets. We have a saying, if you have bedbugs you have to catch one and pour boiling water into the ear."

Nixon: "We have another saying. This is that the way to kill a fly is to make it drink whisky. But we have a better use for whisky. [Aside] I like to have this battle of wits with the Chairman. He knows his business."

Khrushchev: [manifesting a lack of interest in a data processing machine that answers questions about the United States]: "have heard of your engineers. I am well aware of what they can do. You know for launching our missiles we need lots of calculating machines."

Nixon [hearing jazz music]: "I don't like jazz music."

Khrushchev: "I don't like it either."

Nixon: "But my girls like it."

Mr. Nixon apologized for being a "poor host at the exposition and allowing a ceremonial visit to turn into a hot foreign policy discussion."

Khrushchev [apologizing]: "I always speak frankly."

He said he hoped he had not offended Mr. Nixon.

Nixon: "I've been insulted by experts. Everything we say is in good humor."

Khrushchev: "The Americans have created their own image of the Soviet man and think he is as you want him to be. But he is not as you think. You think the Russian people will be dumbfounded to see these things, but the fact is that newly built Russian houses have all this equipment right now. Moreover, all you have to do to get a house is to be born in the Soviet Union. You are entitled to housing. I was born in the Soviet Union. So I have a right to a house. In America, if you don't have a dollar – you have the right to choose between sleeping in a house or on the pavement. Yet you say that we are slaves of communism."

Nixon: "I appreciate that you are very articulate and energetic."

Khrushchev: "Energetic is not the same as wise."

Nixon: "If you were in our Senate, we would call you a filibusterer. You do all the talking and don't let anyone else talk. To us, diversity, the right to choose, the fact that we have 1,000 builders building 1,000 different houses, is the most important thing. We don't have one decision made at the top by one government official. This is the difference."

Khrushchev: "On political problems we will never agree with you. For instance Mikoyan likes very peppery soup. I do not. But this does not mean that we do not get along."

Nixon: "You can learn from us and we can learn from you. There must be a free exchange. Let the people choose the kind of house, the kind of soup, the kind of ideas they want."

Mr. Khrushchev shifted the talk back to washing machines.

Nixon: "We have many different manufacturers and many different kinds of washing machines so that the housewives have a choice."

Khrushchev: [noting Nixon gazing admiringly at young women modeling bathing suits and sports clothes] "You are for the girls too."

Nixon [indicating a floor sweeper that works by itself and other appliances]: "You don't need a wife."

Khrushchev chuckled.

Nixon: "We do not claim to astonish the Russian people. We hope to show our diversity and our right to choose. We do not wish to have decisions made at the top by government officials who say that all homes should be built in the same way. Would it not be better to compete in the relative merits of washing machines than in the strength of rockets. Is this the kind of competition you want?"

Khrushchev: "Yes that's the kind of competition we want. But your generals say: Let's compete in rockets. We are strong and we can beat you.' But in this respect we can also show you something."

Nixon: "To me you are strong and we are strong. In some ways, you are stronger. In others, we are stronger. We are both strong not only from the standpoint of weapons but from the standpoint of will and spirit. Neither should use that strength to put the other in a position where he in effect has an ultimatum. In this day and age that misses the point. With modern weapons it does not make any difference if war comes. We both have had it."

Khrushchev: "For the fourth time I have to say I cannot recognize my friend Mr. Nixon. If all Americans agree with you then who don't we agree [with]? This is what we want."

Nixon: "Anyone who believes the American Government does not reflect the people is not an accurate observer of the American scene. I hope the Prime Minister understands all the implications of what I have just said. Whether you place either one of the powerful nations or any other in a position so that they have no choice but to accept (sic) or fight, then you are playing with the most destructive force in the world. This is very important in the present world context. It is very dangerous. When we sit down at a conference table it cannot put an ultimatum to another. It is impossible. But I shall talk to you about this later."

Khrushchev: "If you have raised the questions, why not go on with it now while the people are listening? We know something about politics, too. Let your correspondents compare watches and see who is filibustering. You put great emphasis on diktat' [dictation]. Our country has never been guided by diktat'. Diktat' is a foolish policy."

Nixon: "I am talking about it in the international sense."

Khrushchev: "It sounds to me like a threat. We, too, are giants. You want to threaten we will answer threats with threats."

Nixon: "Who wants to threaten?"

Khrushchev: "You are talking about implications. I have not been. We have the means at our disposal. Ours are better than yours. It is you who want to compete. Da, da, da."

Nixon: "We are well aware of that. To me who is best is not material."

Khrushchev: "You raised the point. We want peace and friendship with all nations, especially with America."

Nixon: "We want peace too and I believe that you do also."

Khrushchev: "Yes, I believe that."

Nixon: "I see that you want to build a good life. But I don't think that the cause of peace is helped by reminders that you have greater strength than us because that is a threat too."

Khrushchev: "I was answering your words. You challenged me. Let's argue fairly."

Nixon: "My point was that in today's world it is immaterial which of the two great countries at any particular moment has the advantage. In war, these advantages are illusory. Can we agree on that."

Khrushchev: "Not quite. Let's not beat around the bush."

Nixon: "I like the way he talks."

Khrushchev: "We want to liquidate all bases from foreign lands. Until that happens, we will speak different languages. One who is for putting an end to bases on foreign lands is for peace. One who is against it is for war. We have liquidated our forces and offered to make a peace treaty and eliminate the point of friction in Berlin. Until we settle that question, we will talk different languages."

Nixon: "Do you think it can be settled at Geneva?"

Khrushchev: "If we considered it otherwise, we would not have incurred the expense of sending our foreign minister to Geneva. [Foreign minister Andrei A.] Gromyko is not an idler. He is a very good man."

Nixon: "We have great respect for Mr. Gromyko. Some people say he looks like me.
I think he is better looking. I hope it [the Geneva conference] will be successful."

Khrushchev: "It does not depend on us."

Nixon: "It takes two to make an agreement. You cannot have it all your own way."

Khrushchev: "These are questions that have the same aim. To put an end to the vestiges of war, to make a peace treaty with Germany – that is what we want. It is very bad that we quarrel over the question of war and peace."

Nixon: "There is no question but that your people and you want the government of the United States being for peace; anyone who thinks that it is not for peace is not an accurate observer of America. In order to have peace, Mr. Prime Minister, even in an argument between friends, there must be sitting down around a table. There must be discussion. Each side must find areas where it looks at the other's point of view. The world looks to you today with regard to Geneva. I believe it would be a grave mistake and a blow to peace if it were allowed to fail."

Khrushchev: "The two sides must seek ways of agreement."

Sketches Martí Guixé

Martí is a talented communicator. His drawings are like a movie. On the following pages you will find a selection of drawings he did for several projects. No captions, no explanations, just some communicative drawings (and some images).

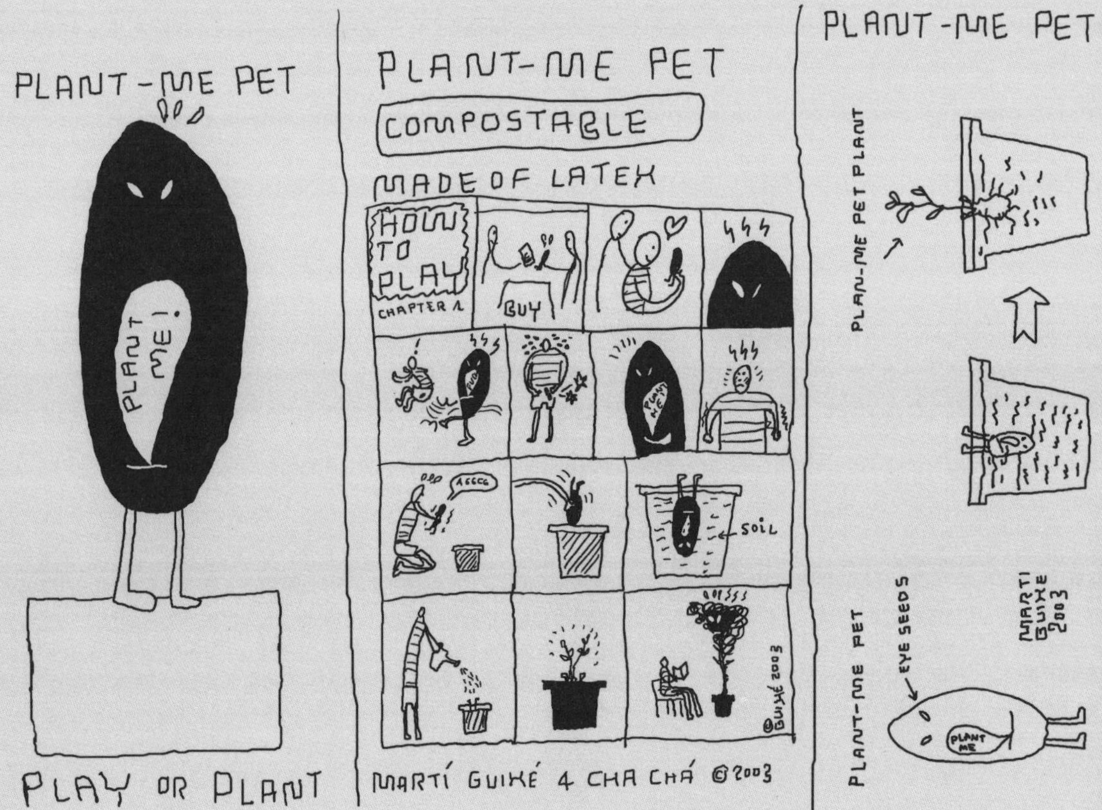
PLANT-ME PET
PLANT ME!
PLAY OR PLANT
PLANT-ME PET
COMPOSTABLE
MADE OF LATEX
HOW TO PLAY
CHAPTER 1
BUY
SOIL
MARTÍ GUIXÉ 4 CHA CHÁ ©2003
PLANT-ME PET
PLAN-ME PET PLANT
PLANT-ME PET
EYE SEEDS
PLANT ME
MARTI GUIXE 2003

141 BRIGHT MINDS, BEAUTIFUL IDEAS

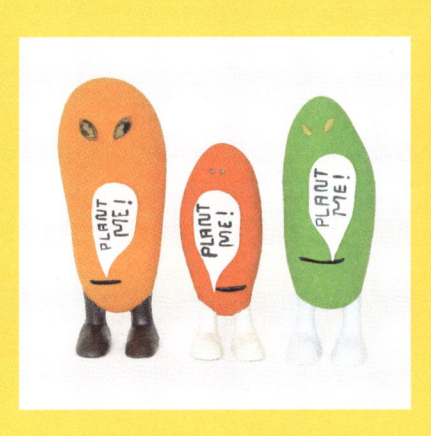

142 BRIGHT MINDS, BEAUTIFUL IDEAS

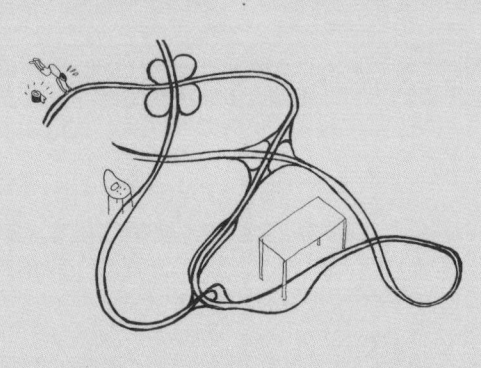

CONFIGURE YOUR OWN NET

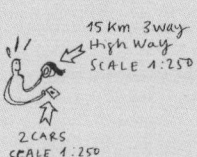

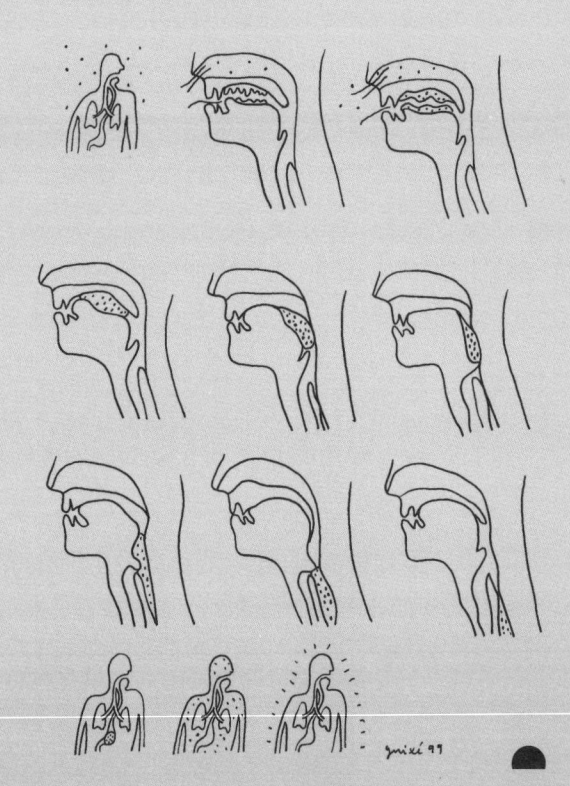

AUTOBAND KIT
OPEN IT.
15 Km 3way Highway SCALE 1:250
2 CARS SCALE 1:250

HOW TO PLAY:
Stick Autoband on any SURFACE
DO TRUMPETS...
CLOVERLEAFS

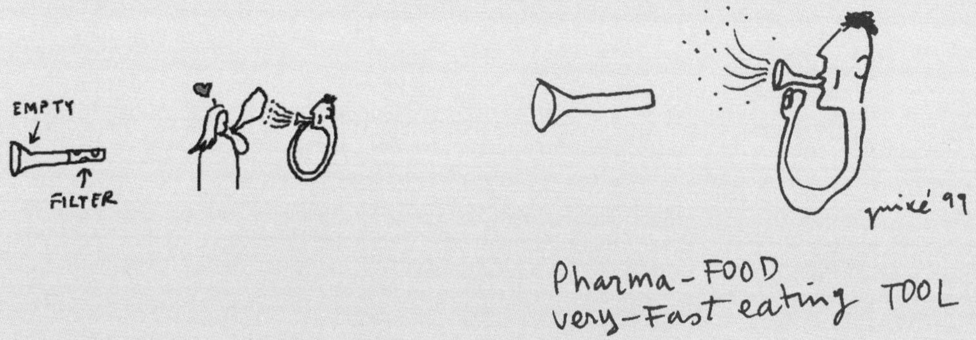

143 BRIGHT MINDS, BEAUTIFUL IDEAS

EMPTY
FILTER

Pharma-FOOD
very-Fast eating TOOL

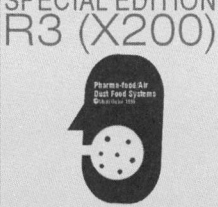

guixé 99

PHARMA-SPAMT
SPECIAL EDITION
R3 (X200)

How to eat PHARMA-SPAMT

ENTER Pharma-Bar — Smell — SALiva Activates — Breath Continuously — Traga SALIVA — AURA Comes

guixé '99

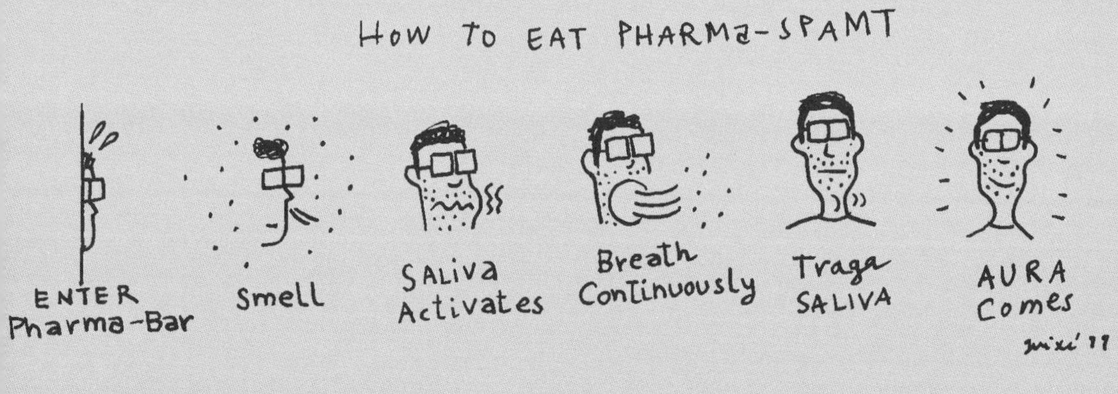

144 BRIGHT MINDS, BEAUTIFUL IDEAS

145 BRIGHT MINDS, BEAUTIFUL IDEAS

position NORMAL

--WARNING--
HIGH NUTRIENT
AIR ZONE
Pharma FOOD / ©Martí Guixé 1999

--ATENCIÓ--
ZONA AMB ALTA
CONCENTRACIÓ DE
NUTRIENTS A L'AIRE
Pharma FOOD / ©Martí Guixé 1999

Martí Guixé 1999

--ATENCIÓ--
ZONA AMB ALTA
CONCENTRACIÓ DE
NUTRIENTS A L'AIRE
Pharma FOOD / ©Martí Guixé 1999

--ATENCION--
ZONA CON ALTA
CONCENTRACION DE
NUTRIENTES EN EL AIRE
Pharma FOOD / ©Martí Guixé 1999

--ATENCIÓ--
ZONA AMB ALTA
CONCENTRACIÓ DE
NUTRIENTS A L'AIRE
Pharma FOOD / ©Martí Guixé 1999

--ATENCION--
ZONA CON ALTA
CONCENTRACION DE
NUTRIENTES EN EL AIRE
Pharma FOOD / ©Martí Guixé 1999

parental advice:

WARNING!

playing with **autoband,** children learn abstract concepts such as "lobbing" "politics" "ecology" "public opinion" "territory".

---WARNING---
YOU ARE ENTERING
HIGH NUTRIENT AIR ZONE

Pharma FOOD / © Martí Guixé 1999

Pictures by Martí Guixé
In a period of about two months Martí made (while travelling, working and socializing) pictures of objects, society and work in progress. A selection of these images are printed in this book.

8 pages with 30 pictures, made by Martí Guixé

Lausanne-Mudac

Lausanne-Center

Barcelona-Hardware_shop

Lausanne-Mudac_press_conference

Barcelona-Modelista Duran (by modelmaker)

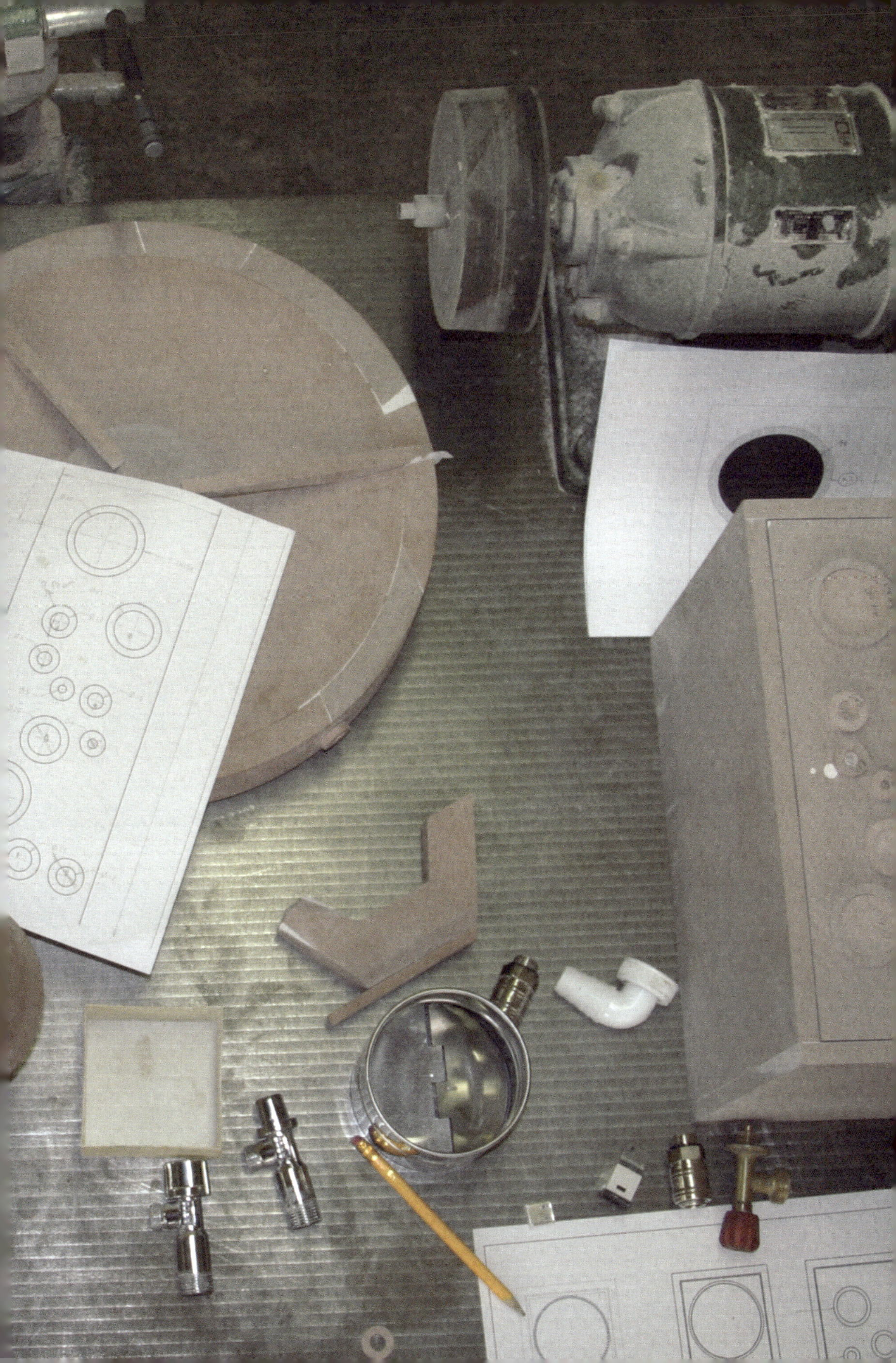

Barcelona-Barna pint (By industrial Painter)

Barcelona-Modelista Duran (by modelmaker)

Barcelona-Barna pint (By industrial Painter)

Barcelona-Modelista Duran (by modelmaker)

Barcelona, my day by the photo shooting

Unknown

Barcelona-science museum

elona-by the future Food culture museum

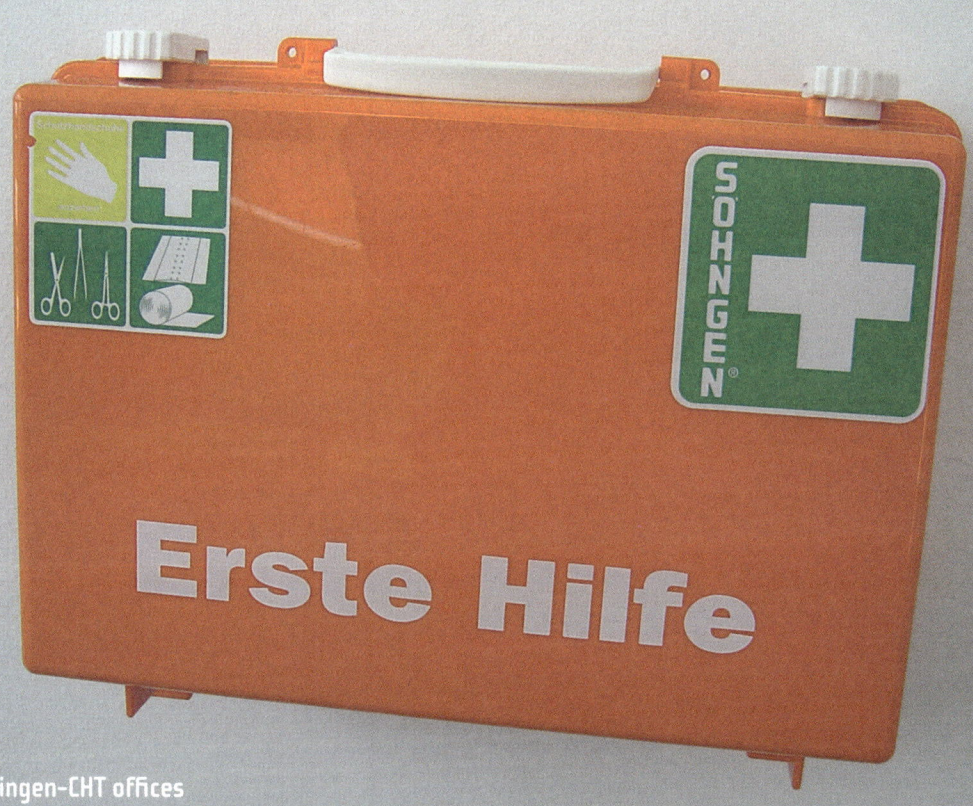

Thübingen-CHT offices

Mallorca Airport

Barcelona_by a tapas Bar

Lausanne_by a bar

Barcelona_passeig de Gracia

Mallorca airport

Madrid_Desigual future showroom

Madrid_by a bar in the center

North Italy, highway

Mallorca_by the coast

PlayStation

Barcelona_Calabria with Corcega

Lausanne_by breakfast

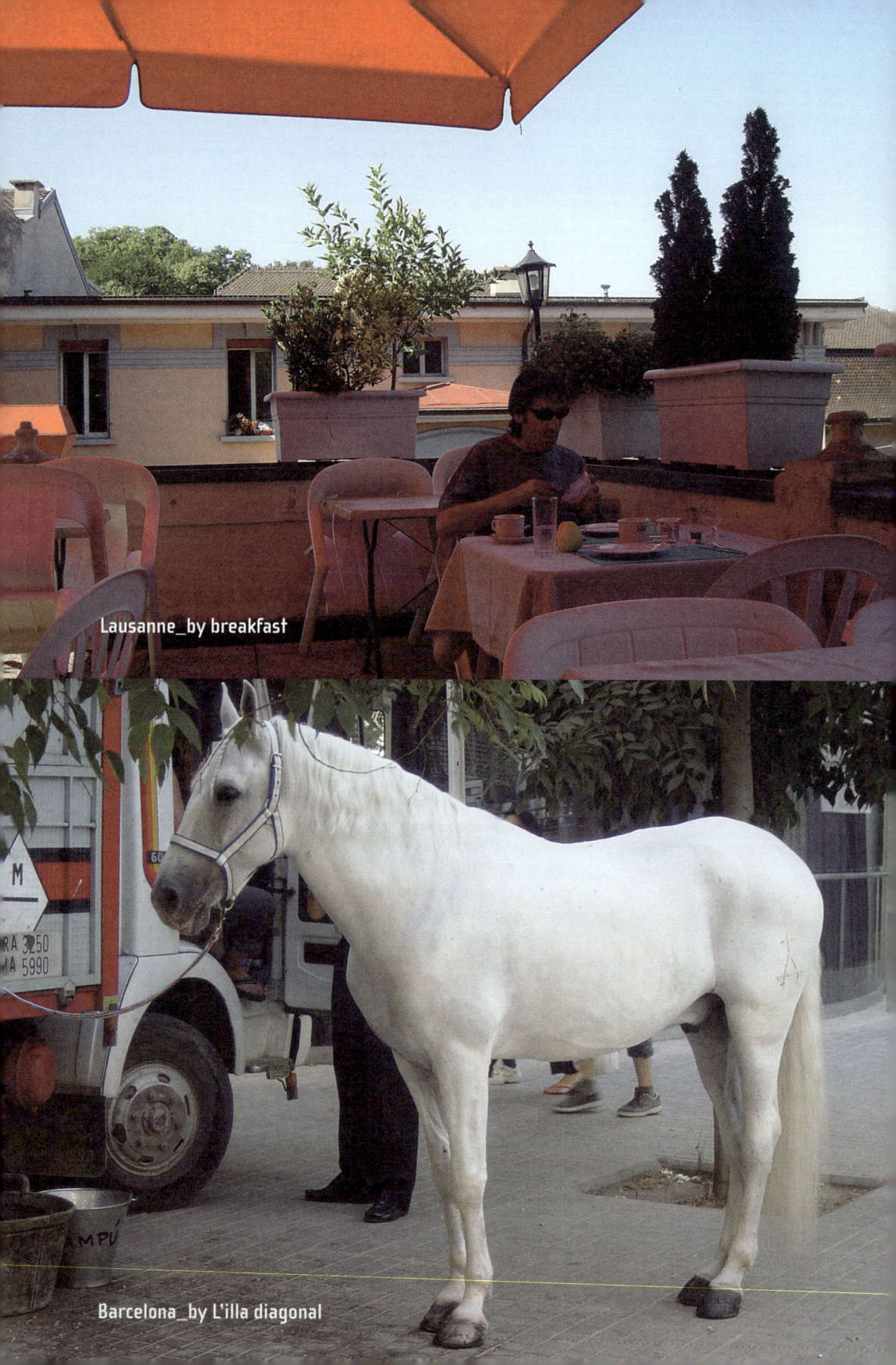

Barcelona_by L'illa diagonal

Barcelona_Sant Jordi

Sant Carlos de la Rapita_beach

Timeline 1969-2003

What was happening in the world in the last years. We made a selection of influential political events, happenings, discoveries and inventions since 1969 until today. (August 17th, 2003)

Timeline 1969-2003

1969: Mass tourism starts to boom.

1971: Floppy disk and microprocessor invented. *Médecins Sans Frontières* was founded.

1972: President Nixon visits China. Bloody attacks by the PLO and Rote Armee Fraktion (RAF). 'The Limits to Growth', the Club of Rome report, that warns against the negative impact of the consumer society.

1973: The US stop war negotiations in North Vietnam. The international oil crisis stimulates the development of atomic energy. Genetic technology begins to develop.

1974: End of the dictatorships in Portugal and Greece are removed. American research concludes that propellants are responsible for the hole in the ozone layer.

1975: End of the Spanish dictatorship. South Vietnam capitulates and the country is reunited. Civil war in Ethiopia, Lebanon and Angola. The first D-I-Y construction kits are launched on the US market.

1976: Arrests in China after the death of Mao. The first electronic word processors appear on the New York and Cologne stock exchanges. Concorde launches its trans-Atlantic service.

1977: President Sadat of Egypt visits Israel on a peace mission. Apple sells the first personal computers. Smallpox is wiped out. Registration of the first AIDS patients.

1978: First G7 summit on the world economy. First test-tube baby. Evidence that radioactivity filters into the food chain.

1979: The Soviet Union attacks Afghanistan. In Persia the Shah is deposed and the Islamic Republic of Iran is founded under Ayatollah Khomeini. Uganda deposes dictator Idi Amin. First cellular phone communication network starts in Japan.

1980: First Gulf War between Iran and Iraq. Large-scale race riots in South Africa. The death of Tito endangers the unity of Yugoslavia.

1981: Anwar Sadat assassinated. Discovery of the AIDS virus. IBM sells its first laptop computers. MTV America goes on air – its first video clip is 'Video killed the radiostar'.

1982: Falklands war between England and Argentina. The US firm Compaq markets the first PC clone.

1983: A UNO commission calculates that the South American countries are in debt to the tune of 275 billion US dollars.

1984: Union Carbide disaster in Bhopal, India. First CD players launched on the market.

1985: Israel pulls out of Lebanon. The EC gradually introduces catalyst converters to cars. Live Aid, a pop concert to raise money for the famine in Ethiopia is the biggest mega-event ever, broadcast in 160 countries. The wreck of the Titanic is found.

1986: The US replies to terrorist attacks with an air attack on Libya. A large-scale economic boycott of South Africa begins. The nuclear power plan at Chernobyl, the Ukraine, explodes.

1987: The world is euphoric about the reforms introduced by Russian President Gorbachev. The Israeli occupied territories begin the Intifada. The US begins to develop the Global Positioning System (GPS). Proof of the existence of the hole in the ozone layer.

1988: Large-scale political reforms in Hungary prelude the end of communism. House music enters the scene: huge parties and use of XTC (Ecstasy) mark a period of growing hedonism in the wealthy countries.

1989: The fall of the Berlin Wall signals the end of communism. Free elections in Hungary, Czechoslovakia and Romania. In Beijing, China, mass student protests for liberalization are violently subdued on Tiananmen Square. Disturbances begin in Kosovo, Yugoslavia.

1990: USSR becomes Russia with Letland, Estland, Lithuania as independent states. Iraq invades Kuwait. Namibia is the last independent African country. Nelson Mandela is freed after 27 years.

1991: Civil war in Yugoslavia. UNO army frees Kuwait; Iraq retreats, leaving burning oil wells.

1992: Caucasian states demand the return of their independence. South Africa announces the end of apartheid. The Treaty of Maastricht stipulates that the European Community will henceforth be known as the European Union and that an Economic and Monetary Union (EMU) will be formed with the Euro as currency. In 'Jihad vs. MacWorld', Benjamin Barber describes mounting resistance to globalisation.

1993: First free elections in Russia. International terrorism takes hold in America with an attack on the World Trade Center, New York. The Mosaic programme, the first browser to allow graphic surfing, heralds the breakthrough of the World Wide Web.

1994: American planes bomb Serb camps in Yugoslavia. Bloody ethnic conflict in Rwanda. Russia invades Chechnya. In South Africa's first free elections, Nelson Mandela is voted President. The Channel Tunnel is opened in Europe.

1995: Yitzhak Rabin is assassinated. The free border traffic outlined in the Schengen Convention is finally introduced in 7 EU countries. Environmental activities hamper the sinking of the Shell-dumped oilrig Brent Spar.

1996: Swiss banks are discredited when they are shown to still have 7 billion DM in their possession. There are now an estimated 22.6 millio AIDS victims. The Petronas Towers in Kuala Lumpur beats the Sears Tower in Chicago as highest building. The LCD screen and digital radio are discovered.

1997: Dolly the sheep is the first identical genetic copy (clone) of an adult mammal. The former British colony Hong Kong is 'handed back' to China. The tobacco industry is prohibited from advertising. The Guggenheim Museum in Balboa opens. Kevin Kelly publishes 'New Rules for the New Economy'.

1998: France introduces the 35-hour working week.

1999: 'Anti-globalists' are in the news with protests against the WTO summit in Seattle. Fears of a 'millennium bug' assume bizarre proportions. The latest movie in the 'Star Wars' trilogy is the most profitable movie ever, through merchandising alone. The highpoint of the Internet bubble: the USA now have 14 Internet billionaires and a share in Internet bookshop Amazon.com rises 70 times in value in 2.5 years although it makes a loss of 390 million guilders this year.

2000: Austria is the first country after the Second World War to elect a right-wing government. In Zimbabwe black Africans occupy white farmlands with government approval.

Microsoft is sued for abusing its dominant power position. Fatal accident rings the death toll for Concorde. European Commission approval sanctions the world's greatest merger between America Online and Time Warner.

2001: The first BSE and Foot-and-Mouth crisis in Europe since 1897. The Taliban regime destroys statues belonging to the world's cultural heritage in Afghanistan. Two planes crash into the World Trade Center in New York; the Twin Towers collapse. Terrorist leader Osama Bin Laden is the presumed instigator.

2002: US President Bush launches a worldwide 'War Against Terrorism'. Fraud is the cause of the largest bankruptcy in Amercan history: the energy giant Enron. Introduction of the Euro.

2003: Invasion of Iraq.

Jurgen Bey

A-056
MACFRIES
FUNDAÇÃO DAS DESCOBERTAS
CENTRO CULTURAL DE BELEM

Jurgen Bey

Jurgen Bey (1965) is driven by the ambition to understand the world. He is able to question it in a unique manner. According to him, wanting to think or create something new is bizarre, for every thing or solution we can possibly dream of does already exist in the world around us. It is just a question of recognizing it and then of being able to translate it into something people want to use. Therefore, Bey is continuously busy analyzing the real qualities and hidden values of phenomena and things around us. He even analyses phenomena like dust or waiting, that no-one else is interested in but which could be of huge value – as soon as we understand how to use it.
Being deeply interested in the emotional meaning of things, Bey creates new images and works that provoke thinking and discussions about the value of the contemporary production machine. Besides its plain functionality his conceptual work is part of the international discussion around the role of design and the designer.

Jurgen Bey sees stories as collector's items – stories old and new, fanciful and prosaic, unremembered tales and sagas still waiting to be told. With a little bit of luck and a lot of thinking and trying, he's able to translate these narratives into functional objects. When he and a dozen or so other designers and artists were commissioned by Auping to design products based on the theme 'mobile dreaming', some of his stories suddenly came together in a wondrous way. The story that in certain areas in outer space – regions called 'black holes' – the same little spoon, normally light as a feather, is staggeringly heavy, and the one of the snail, lugging its shell around for a lifetime. In Bey's design a simple operation is all it takes for dresses and costumes to balloon within seconds into high-rise proportions to reveal unsuspected (dream)scapes. Having finished the project for Auping, Bey is already contemplating the idea of complete dwellings so light and so small (before expanding) that they fit into the palm of a human hand.
In the early '90s Bey attended the Academy of Industrial Design in Eindhoven (currently the Design Academy). The Dutch organization Droog Design promoted his work from the very beginning. Along with a handful of young colleagues (like Jan Konings, Tejo Remy, Hella Jongerius and Marcel Wanders) Bey was to shape the image of Dutch design on an international level during the last decade. Their designs were noteworthy by the unconventional mentality they expressed. Neither a user-friendly attitude nor the purely formal or aesthetic aspects of a product determine its design. What counts more than anything else are underlying ideas, humor and down-to-earth simplicity. In the products that Bey has designed and realized since that time – on his own or, in a few cases, with others – the story he's eager to tell is always at least as essential as pure functionality. Some of his designs would not be out of place in the context of art.

'Soul' may not be a term that Bey uses to describe an inanimate phenomenon, but he does approach things as if each embodies a variable quality all its own. Moviemakers often use the same idea in their films; the objects featured in Charlie Chaplin films have many a human characteristic and in the movie 'Crouching Tiger, Hidden Dragon' gravity is defied in such a convincing way that many a spectator fancies to be able to ascend after it has finished – if only for a second. For a designer it is an exciting idea that not only people, but also objects, are suddenly not what he thought they were – weightless, for example. Bey desires to translate his amazement at the world by all means into functional objects. In the end most of life's stories are found in the items we use every day.

Bey layers old stories, one atop the other, and transforms them into something new. This happens quite literally in his 'Kokon'-series. Various objects – chair-cum-table, chair-cum-lamp – are trapped beneath a shared skin made of a stretchy synthetic material. Archetypal forms, familiar to all, protrude from the thin, resilient skin, revealing their original identity and history; symbiotically united, they tell a brand-new story.

In 'Broken Family', a dinner service of which the glaze connects disparate pieces in a wonderful way, the skin plays an even greater role. A high-gloss layer of silver eliminates the imperfections of cups without handles and cracked plates and unites them in a new family.
'Tree Trunk Bench' and 'Lamp Shade' both hide several storylines as well. By casting the backrests of old chairs in bronze and placing them side by side on a felled tree trunk, nature and culture enter into a miraculous cross fertilization. And as soon as the lamp in 'Lamp Shade' is switched on, the old chandelier that hides behind the semi-transparent synthetic shade becomes visible. The modern lamp stands out best when the past lights up; if the object does not function we see nothing but untransparent contemporary design without roots, a closed universe.

In his search for the very essence of a subject and of hidden meanings, Bey relates to scientists who question reality, both visible and invisible, down through the ages and take neither nature nor human evolution for granted. He sees significant differences between his work and theirs, however. While a scientist's goal lies in the sensation of answers, Bey's aim revolves around the sensation of questioning the existing and being amazed about it. *"Why should I invent something new when reality already offers so many stunning images, stories and extraordinary solutions?"*, he wonders. *"As a designer, all I have to do is find them and transform them into new stories and new products."*

This way he combines pragmatism, common sense and an interest in scientific discovery with an almost childlike passion for fairytales. For the 'Healing'-series Bey removed a part of a leg from a classic chair, an object richly laden with associations. The defect can be corrected by efficiently replacing the leg with a stack of magazines; from the surplus wood he built a toy car. The tabletop of the stove-table, another piece in the same series, seems to face extermination as it seems to disappear, one piece at a time, into the heater. The handicap of one object is the blessing of another. According to Bey, 'Healing' is all about coping with shortcomings. Words like 'handicap' and 'talent' are extremely relative and rely entirely on a circumstantial context. In a gigantic Olympic stadium every eye is on the guy who just ran the 100 metres in no time flat, but by reading lips that one deaf man in the mass can do what nobody else can do: understand what someone well out of earshot is saying. The 'Healing' series eventually became 'Do-Add', a line of products commissioned by Droog Design; for the finishing touch some action of the user is required to restore a possible function. Here, too, the message is: one person's handicap is another person's blessing.

Bey' natural questioning behavior, his interest in environmental issues, human rules and behavior, and his more philosophical approach in design make him an influential and inspiring designer and teacher. As a designer, he can be considered as the most conceptual in the Dutch designers scene and as one of the most striking designers of his time. His office is small, many of his projects are self-initiated. But he cannot complain about the response to his work; even his ideas and unrealized projects are published in magazines all over the world. And there are many realized projects, like the Wedding Room in Utrecht City Hall that combines used and new things in a special way. Like the tactile solutions for the interior architecture of an institute for the blind (in collaboration with Hella Jongerius) and a new shop-window concept for Levi's, in which passers-by can see a glimpse of the products every time the LCD-monitors open on a rhythmic, heart-like beating. A recent project is a part of the interior of the Dutch insurance company Interpolis. Inspired by the history of this company, which was established as a loan-office for farmers, Bey applied rural motives in the covering and upholstery and gave old-fashioned arm-chairs a new shape and function. Referring to the rustic coziness and intimacy of old, he let history steal into this hypermodern company quietly.

An abundance of stories waits to be translated into products. Like the story of the omnipresent dust that could be the new gold, Bey knows for sure – as soon as he manages to find out what the right function is. Everything has a reason and a story behind, even apparently senseless behaviors and phenomena. Everyday life has all the answers, provided that one finds the right questions. Bey's mission is to look for them. Through his eyes the world gains lots of imagination.

Louise Schouwenberg

Cracking the codes of reality
an interview with Jurgen Bey

Ineke Schwartz (IS): *Your way of looking at the world is quite different from that of other people or designers. You puzzle and pore over things that others just don't notice.*

Jurgen Bey (JB): Well, the thing is, I have a certain perspective. I look at things as if they have a life and language of their own. If you do this consistently, the world starts to take on a totally different appearance. And that's what I use as a designer, that way you can make connections that really do lead to new insights. I find this quite easy to do, although I notice that for some others it's hard. Things also pose their own questions. In India, everything is covered in a fine dust. What's the purpose of dust? If I can puzzle out the answer to that, I've made a fortune. And why are there so many borderliners, people on the fringes of society, people who miss the boat. There must be some point to all this. These questions are like crossword puzzles. I go looking for patterns; when I discover the code, I can apply it to some other problem and see if I come up with a solution. I'm continually being astonished by things. And when everyone is convinced something is no good I'm still wondering whether it doesn't have a certain value. It only works if you really take a question seriously. I think that's my secret. The only problem is that it never stops. Sometimes I've really had enough for a while of the constant, unending business of seeing, pondering, puzzling about things.

IS: *So why do you do it?*
JB: I can't help myself, I'm trying to understand the world. Also, I believe in pure goodness and that nothing is without meaning. Everything has a value, provided it appears in the right place at the right time. It's a matter of recognizing that value, that quality, and then to transform it into something that can be used. If you come across something valuable and tuck it away in your metaphorical suitcase there's sure to come a moment when you can make use of it. I find evolution an important notion too and I try to place things in such a way that they can grow and evolve.

IS: *'Your metaphorical suitcase' filled with materials – that's what you carry with you as a designer? What does this imply for your work?*
JB: As a designer I feel like an explorer, asking questions, making connections, returning full of stories after a long journey – stories that in my case are products. Being a designer is also like threading beads on a string – you have a theory and so you take a certain route and follow it, making use of the things you've collected on the way. You make new beginnings over and over again, and you are very aware of the strengths of your work, and some beads are threaded side by side that never appeared in this combination before, and a spark ignites. This requires a certain way of looking at things and you develop it by examining everything around you, asking a great many questions and spending lots of time looking at works of art.

IS: *Give me an example of an object that developed from this way of threading beads.*
JB: My Garden House is made of all kinds of odds and ends jumbled up in a different place from where you'd normally find them. Still, they speak a recognizable language. They're just in a different combination from what you'd usually see, so a new world is created consisting of things we recognize. Building sheds, sleeping under the starry sky or in a solid bed – everyone's knows what you're talking about when you speak of these things, and they represent a certain feeling. It's interesting that if I put the same odds and ends in a different configuration, no one wants it – although as it now is, people are keen to have it and will pay a lot for it. That's it, you see – you can make money from all kinds of things so long as you go about it in the right way.

IS: *You talk a lot about India. Apart from its tourist appeal, what attracts you there?*
JB: I discovered all kinds of qualities in India that have become utterly obscured here in the West. Since being in India I've noticed a few gaps in the world: things that are there but that no one thinks about, that aren't developed or studied.

You notice straight away, for instance, that there's far too much traffic, a poor infrastructure, a poor sewage system. As a good Westerner your hands itch to widen the streets, to install a sound sewage pipe, in short – to spread a layer of general utility. In our world everything has to happen wearing seven-league boots but when millions of people live in a certain may, you can assume you'll find qualities that have their use. And as a designer, you can cultivate quality. For instance, I see someone spending hours gouging out grass from between tiles using a chisel; there must be some point to this, if only for the very reason that you can think of hundreds of ways of doing the job quicker and better. Pull the grass out with your hands, man, or get some shears. Back in the Netherlands, and still pondering about the quality of the man with the chisel I notice the same thing is happening here. There's a growing number of help-desks and service-centres, offering all kinds of assistance and advice, while you still have no answer to the first question which you asked them. Because we stand here holding our cellphones we think we're doing something important, but like the man in India we're just wasting, or killing, time. I'm looking for answers in connection with this kind of waste and destruction.

IS: *You also often refer to nature, using it as an example. What does nature mean for you and your work?*
JB: I think of nature as a kind of book of law full of cases and evidence. It's a world that exists and has proved itself without a visible producer. The most absurd things exist in it but they're proved their right to exist. Fish that look as if they have a whole fishhook stuck in their head, ants that have developed into a living storage depot. If a non-thinking system can produce such wondrously beautiful objects we must surely be able to do the same in a thinking world. These are the things that occupy you as a designer – you can use them at the right moment.

IS: *How do you find that right moment?*
JB: You have to analyze where exactly the quality lies and then transform it. It's very important never to imitate; I'm absolutely convinced that it doesn't work when you try to literally copy something that already exists. For instance, when I was designing the interior for the insurance company Interpolis I wanted to refer to the fact that the origins of the firm lay with farmers and market gardeners. The interiors of farmhouses are enormously attractive even though they consist in a cacophony of styles from many different periods – still, the overall result is one of great beauty and harmony. But the minute you copy that literally you get a Hansel-and-Gretel cottage and you know perfectly well that office folk won't want to be seen dead in it. So the idea has to be pared down (and how exactly that works is hard to say; it's largely an intuitive process, often a case of try, try, try again). You want to make a kind of translation while retaining the quality you started with – but then cleaned up and polished, a sophisticated version, something with a structure and order of its own that will appeal to the sense of status of the future users. After all, they're the ones who'll have to live in the building, I will have skedaddled, so it wouldn't be fair just to land them with something I like. So it has to be a grandmother's house but with a fresh breeze blowing through it that will waft away any negative whiffs and ensure that the staff's Opel Vectra won't look out of place when parked in front.

IS: *You claim that this way of working resembles a kind of language. Design as language? How do you rhyme that with the admiration that you mentioned earlier?*
JB: Everything has a voice and speaks its own language. And so design is also a language, subject to rules. If something looks sloppy and grubby, people won't do anything with it; it they think something looks clean they'll accept it. If something is without any quality it won't have any value. A chair is to sit on and that should be evident. Just look how people react when they

think they're being made a fool of. The bad thing about so much design is that it doesn't speak a language, often because the designer calls upon such things as freedom and creativity, which are in fact fallacies. A designer knows how people are going to react, what they will and won't do, you find this out by watching very carefully and testing out your finds and you use your knowledge to seduce the public. The language I speak of has to do with values and it's linked to a culture. For instance, I wouldn't dare use my language for India because I don't know that world at all and when you don't understand a situation you can't offer a solution. I'd be happy to do something in India, mind you, but then in collaboration with people who come from there and without making the assumption that we do it better. This country's such a total mess. Eighty percent of what we make, we throw on the trash heap.

IS: *You seem to like saying how things ought to be, holding a little sermon.*
JB: Yes and no. I really dislike designers who proclaim what people can and can't do. Who say people shouldn't waste so much, that they should be more environmentally friendly and use recycled goods – bullshit. If recycling was the answer it would have happened long ago. If something doesn't work today why on earth do you imagine things are going to change just because you think they should? You have to realize that things are for what they're for. If you think something isn't up to scratch, or doesn't work, well – get lost and stop misusing it. Everyone has their own job and place in the world. I try to fish things out of the deep, make new constructions and show the world my vision. Reality is an incredible jungle. Every problem has its solution, you only have to look at it and ask the right questions.

Ineke Schwartz

Selected works

Conservation

Many products undergo a period in which they are no longer modish or they bore you. They are out of fashion and may no longer show their faces for a number of years. Protected with a new skin they can outlive this period and re-emerge to be welcomed. (JB)

Cocoon furniture, 1999-2002
Existing furniture has been wrapped in an elastic synthetic fibre. The smooth elastic skin gives it an entirely new appearance. By cross-breeding and grafting, products and functions of a different nature are merged and developed into new products. (JB)

Linen-chest-house, 2002

A covered canopied bed for in the garden. A sleeping old useless linen-cupboard in the loft wanted to be a little sleeping-house and together with old blankets and a tabel they became a 'Linen-chest-house'. (JB)

183 BRIGHT MINDS, BEAUTIFUL IDEAS

Broken family, 1999

A collection of left behind ceramics, from friends or flea-market. In spite of their defects they survived. Covered with a layer of silver they become a new family without loosing their own identity. (JB)

Healing project, 1999

Starting-point of the 'Healing' series is the changing process of familiar furniture, its weakness resulting in new meanings. The removal and addition of elements creates different functions; a broken leg becomes a toy. (JB)

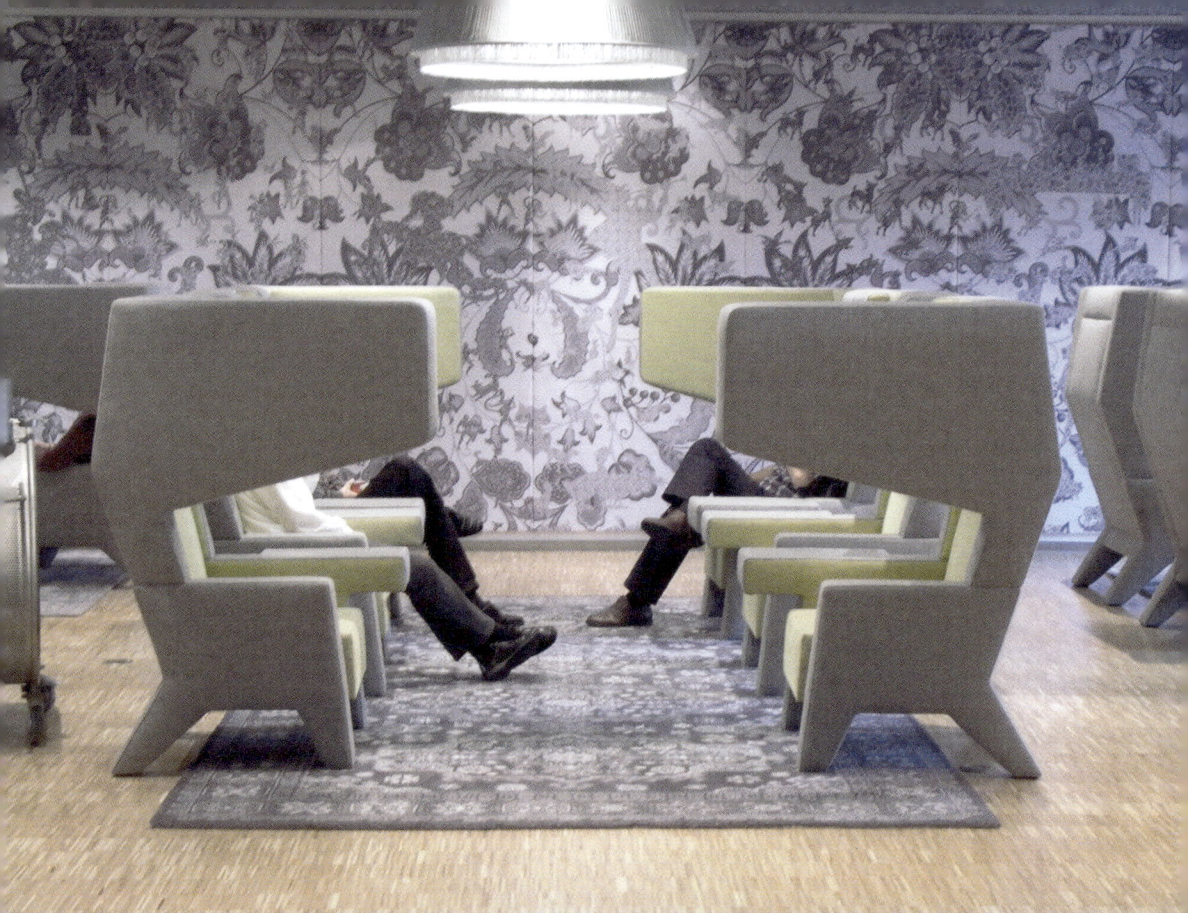

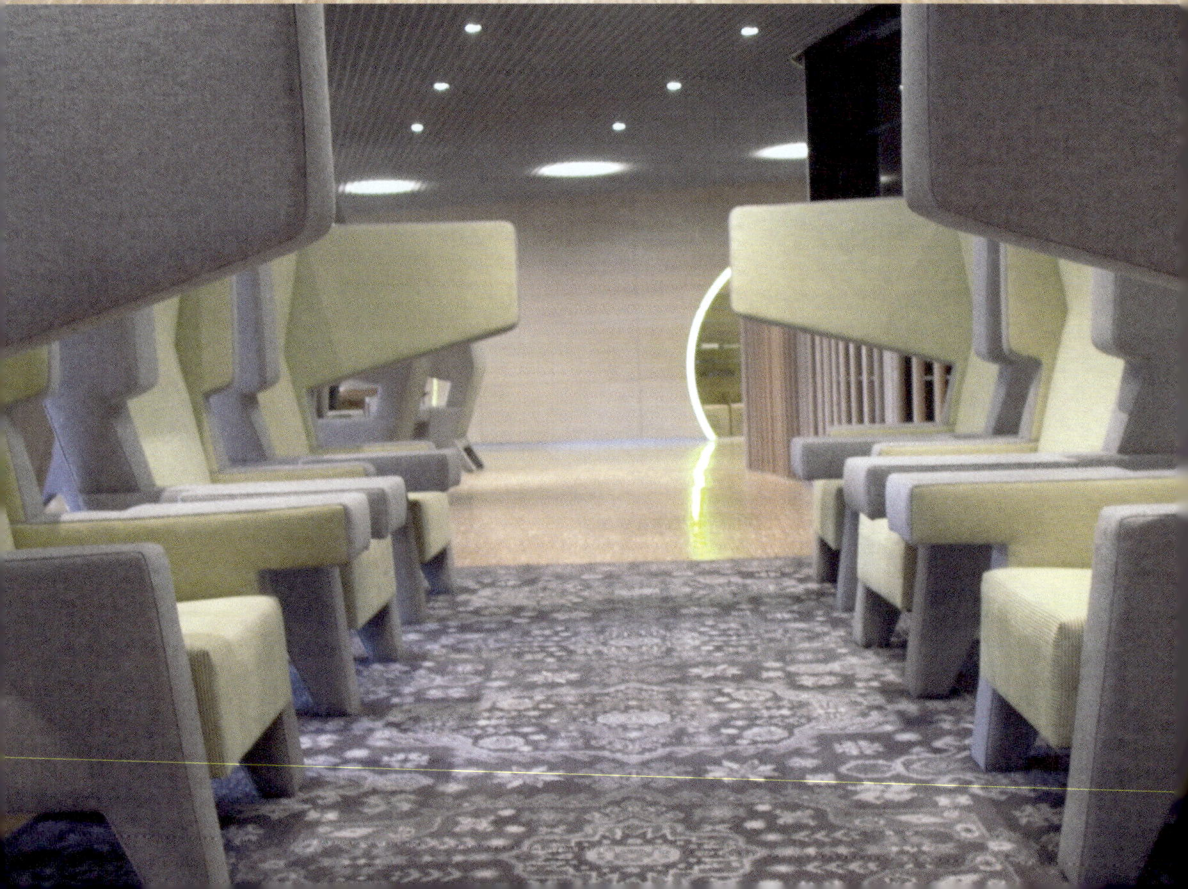

Interpolis, Sits-wallpaper, 2002
Different kind of textiles, used for Dutch costumes, create a patchwork. It looks like a traditional pattern but if you look longer you will discover silhouettes of fairytales in it. (JB)

Interpolis, Ear-chair, 2002
The chairs create a space within a space, due of the size of the ears. The outside of the chairs are gray while the color of the inside varies and gives each 'room' its own character. (JB)

Interpolis, Ceiling-lamp, 2002
Adapted old-fashioned looking ceiling-lamp. TL lights are shining their light through rastered photo's of handpainted ceilings from old Dutch houses which determine the color of the light. (JB)

Interpolis, reception-room, 2002

The function of this room is to receive the customers and to have conferences and little meetings. Interpolis, an indemnity insurance company, finds her roots in the Dutch agrarian world. The reception-rooms are treated like a Sunday-room and designed through out the wealth and beauty the country side interior shows. The interior with its typical furniture, the abundant decorated textiles and strange combinations of this, deformed by time. (JB)

Interpolis, Dutch/Persian-carpet, 2002
Woolen Dutch persians are blown up and roughly woven, looking like a pixeled black and white photo. The measurements of the carpets determine the size of the 'room'. (JB)

Lightshade-shades for Droogdesign, 1999
A new skin which reflect its environment covers an old lamp. Turned on, the lamp gives light, and appears in its old garment to give comfort and character. (JB)

Sketches by Jurgen Bey

Jurgen Bey is a researcher. On the following pages you will find a selection of images and text we took from his concept books as he proposes them to clients and others.

192 BRIGHT MINDS, BEAUTIFUL IDEAS

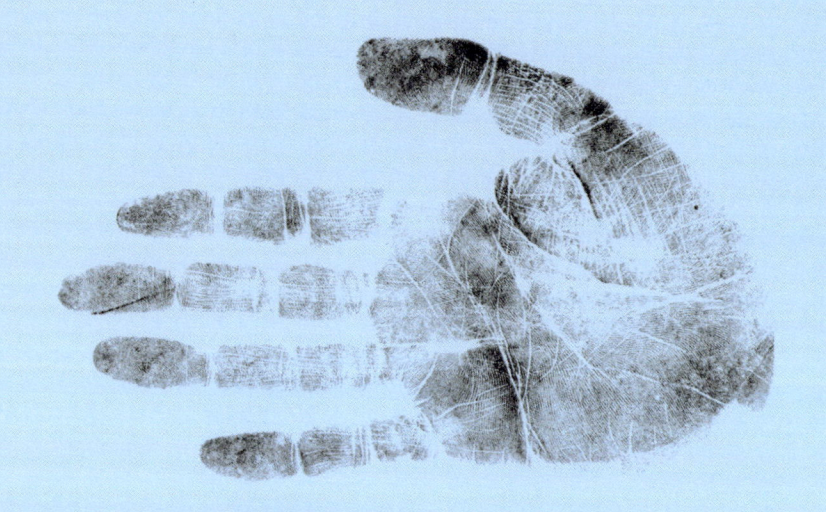

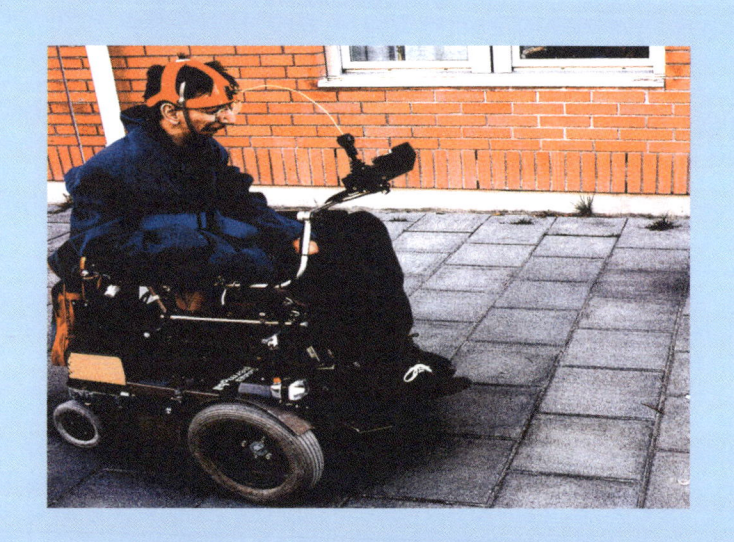

Handwriting

is personal. Although the way they come in to being is exactly the same, there are no two alike. There are aspects of the production process that ensure that they are all unique, so that they have no equivalent in use.

The broken

are disabled and get new instruments, usually to mask their shortcomings. But maybe the wheelchair user is the swiftest messenger, the amputee the strongest mechanic and the deaf the best listeners. New instruments offer new possibilities, new stories and new means of communication.

Communication
between product and user sometimes occurs because the product comes to life. They tell stories. They become individuals that develop good and bad characteristics with beauty and ugliness in function and idleness. They gain characters and speak with their bodies. As with people, the character is laid bare through the unspoken word.

The language
of products is a language that we give them so that they can communicate with users. Sometimes they have an interpreter in the form of a written set of instructions, sometimes through tattoos on their body. It is a functional language that tells us what they can do, where they come from and what they are for.

Maintenance
and protection they can provide for themselves. Fit through exercise, warm through rubbing, hard through labour, cleaning after dirtiness and soft from moisturising.

195 BRIGHT MINDS, BEAUTIFUL IDEAS

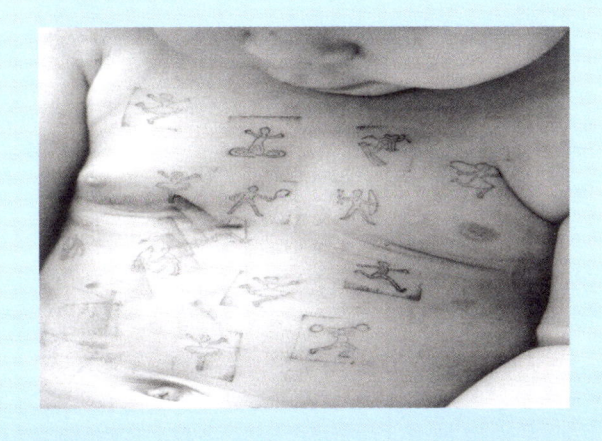

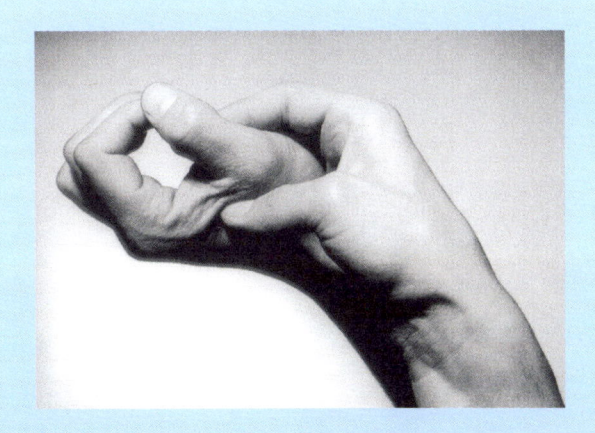

196 BRIGHT MINDS, BEAUTIFUL IDEAS

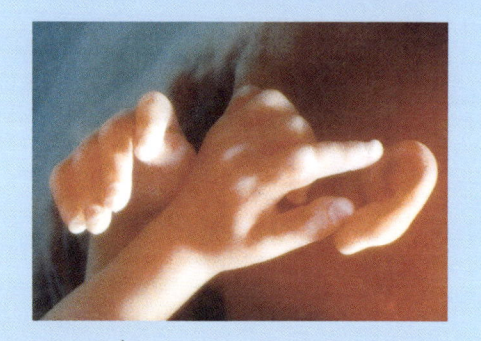

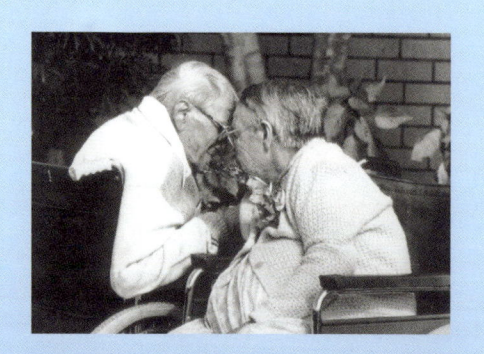

New
the first time, unspoilt, a vulnerable moment. How would it sound, how would it feel? With the first use they are given life. They can do a few things themselves, but they will learn a great deal in order to be able to do it better, and slowly they will gain the habits of their user.

Rafflesia
is the world's largest flower. Considering its size, you would think it would be pollinated by an elephant, but it is pollinated by a fly. Perhaps it is so big to be seen from afar, but in fact the flower seduces with the smell of rotting meat and so could actually be very small. The flower lives parasitically on the root of a tree. A strong jungle giant that requires a lot of food. The flower has won the lottery, has married into wealth and built an enormous castle for itself.

Old age
has come a long way and no longer has to prove itself. They have seen and survived the times. The suppleness and swiftness are gone but movements gain a new form and a personal rhythm. They speak with fragility, if you are careful with me, then I still have much to tell you.

The retiring
are introverted, sparing with their stories.
But they prick our curiosity. You have to make
the effort. They tell their stories only if you really
want to hear and their modesty graces the sounds.

The beetle
with the third eye. The eye is sensitive to
infra-red, on the look-out for a forest fire.
While everything flees from the danger, they
go towards the fire, where they lay their eggs in
charred wood. They have discovered a new world.
An oasis without predators, but with warmth
and new possibilities.

The human body
fascinates me, how it functions, how it reacts
to various situations, how it communicates and
which resources it employs. The aim is to develop
a language for product design and to apply it.

199 BRIGHT MINDS, BEAUTIFUL IDEAS

Made
in order to make. A new world from an old world,
it hands on what it has received, it does what it has
learned and it tells what it has seen.
The hand-made hand makes.

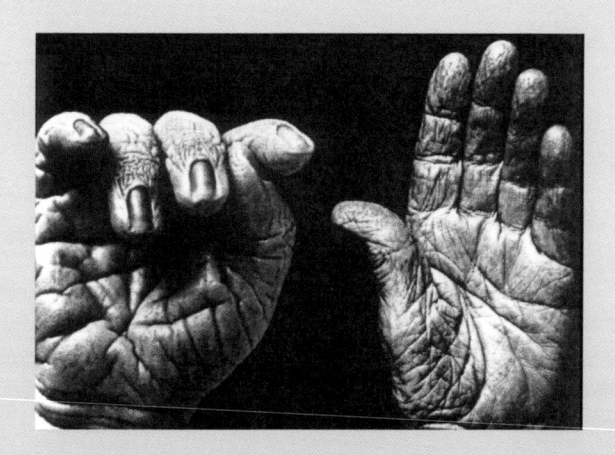

The life

of the hand is my subject of study. The human tool, the user and the origin of almost every product. The developments that they go through, the things they experience, which they form and make unique. On the basis of the capacity for adaptation I want to discover if I can transfer this to products. So that from certain processes, an identical product becomes unique, with specific talents and shortcomings tailored to its use, user and environment.

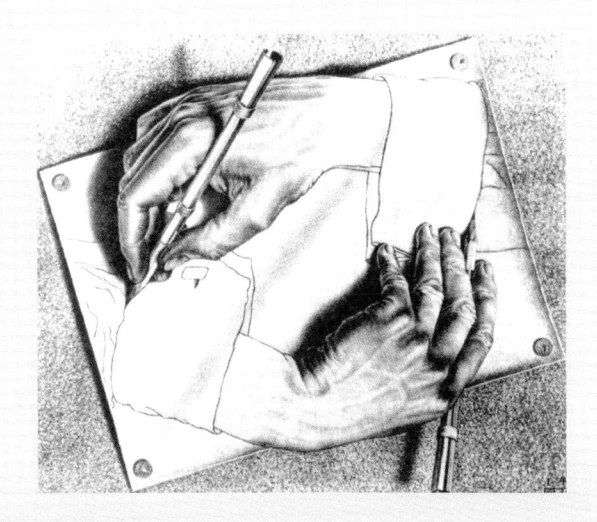

The old

has the same fragility as the new. With the new it was the unscratched, the possible developments, the magic of the first time. With the old it is the drawn, the lived through, the brittleness of possibly the last time.

The use
of products is an extension of the body. Prostheses
that offer new possibilities. A larger eye that can
see the world's news, an electronic mouth that
can make orchestral music, a stomach that can
preserve food, a 100 degree hand that irons.
Instruments that interact with their user and
environment to give pleasure.

Friendship
is a bond of affection that grows from an
intensive period of exploring the world together.
Through acquaintance, exploration, recognition
and acknowledgement a trust develops,
a personal language in which small things become
important. There originates a personal form of
communication without explanation, in which
words, gestures, silences, texts acquire their own
significance.

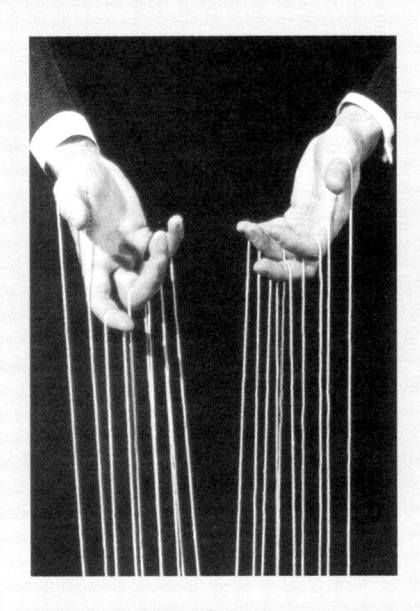

The place
of use calls for adaptation. They absorb their environment and react. Rough work and they become hard, practice and they become nimble-fingered, cold and the hairs stand on end, wet and they wrinkle, much sun and they tan. They tell where they come from, what they are capable of and what they have done.

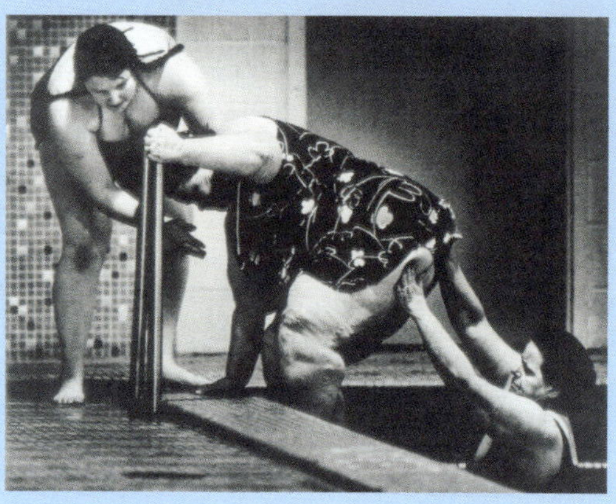

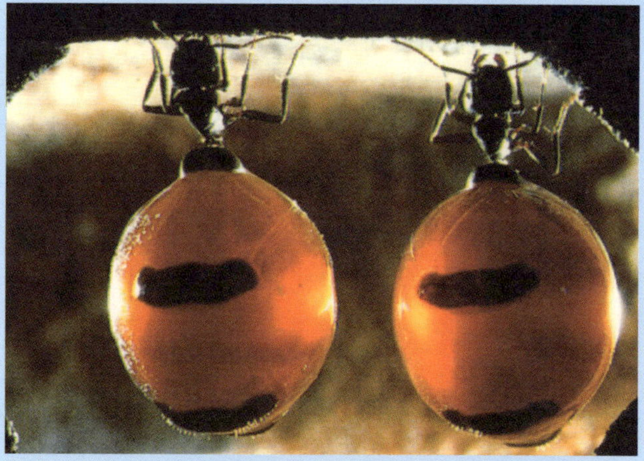

Difference
is not always accepted, but sometimes gains a
very different significance through familiarity.
So-called ugliness attains an unmatched beauty if,
for example, it is your aunt, who used to read you
wonderful stories in which you could luxuriate,
and who created situations that you could share
only with her.

An ant
whose belly has grown into a living larder.
A honey harvest for the whole population, where
the food is kept in perfect condition. Never eat
alone again, always in company and you can literally talk with your mouth full.

Pictures by Jurgen Bey

In a period of about two months Jurgen made (while travelling, working and socializing) pictures of objects, society, work in progress and work in concept. A selection of these images (and some older ones) are printed in this book.

5 pages with 22 pictures, made by Jurgen Bey

Rotterdam / studio / storage

Rotterdam / studio / kitchen

studio / try-out

Rotterdam / studio / making of

The Netherlands / Westerhoven / workshop / execution of design

The Netherlands / Westerhoven / workshop / execution of design

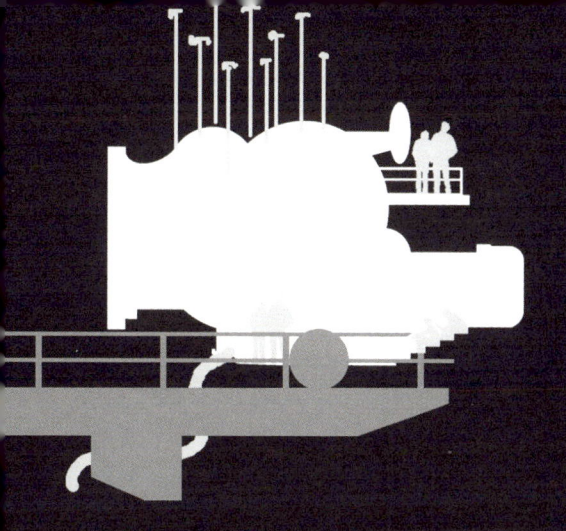

The Netherlands / Eindhoven / Technical University / presentation of design

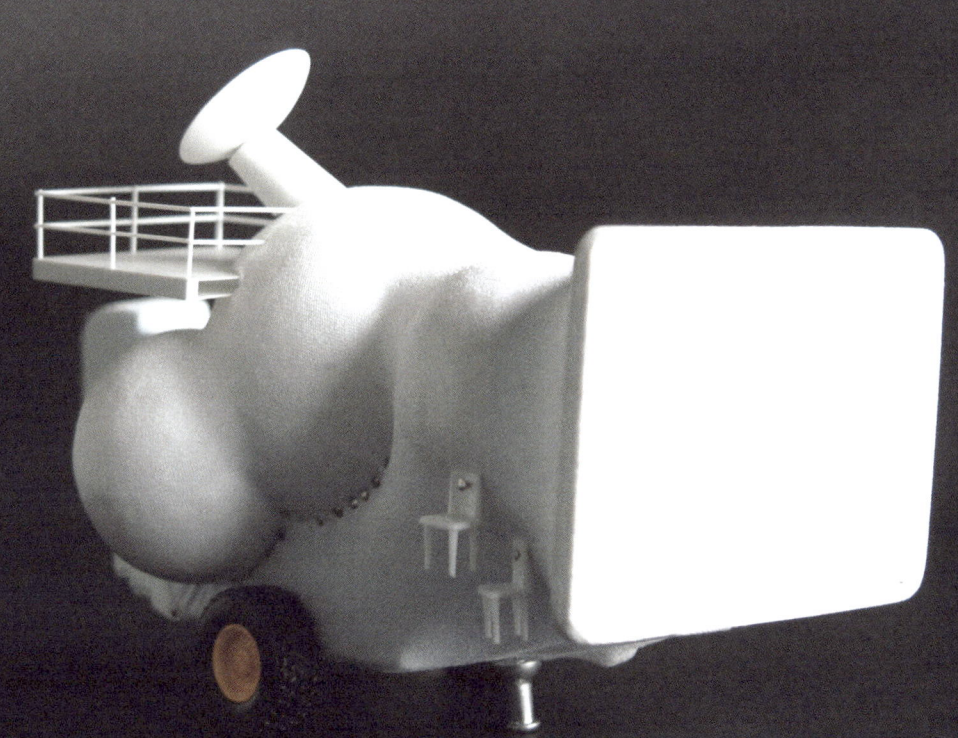

The Netherlands / Eindhoven / Technical University / presentation of design

U.S.A. / Maine / road to Canada / dumpstore

U.S.A. / Maine / road to Canada / boatbuilder

India / road to Udaipur / transport

India / Hyderabad / festivity

France / Paris / School of Arts / exhibition

The Netherlands / Gorssel / farmyard

Portugal / Lisbon / marketplace

Portugal / Lisbon / fishshop

U.S.A. / Washington / shopping mall

India / Bombay / busstop

The Netherlands / Nunspeet / Eibertjesdag

Portugal / Lisbon / marketplace

'Beyond Consumption, Bright Minds' workshop
Centro de Exposições Centro Cultural de Belém –
Bienal de Lisboa, Lisbon, Portugal
From 19th to 23rd May 2003

Eighteen students from 9 design academies from 4 countries were invited to join a workshop with the theme 'Beyond consumption', led by Martí Guixé and Jurgen Bey.
The goal of this five-day workshop was to create ideas based on local values (Jurgen Bey) and on global thinking (Martí Guixé).

Martí Guixé

WORK
SHOP

Jurgen Bey

PARTICIPATING SCHOOLS AND STUDENTS

Faculdade de Belas Artes de Lisboa, Lisbon, Portugal
Daniel Teles Caramelo

Escola Superior de Tecnologia, Gestão, Arte e Design, Caldas da Rainha, Portugal
João Sabino

Instituto de Artes Visuais, Design e Marketing, Lisbon, Portugal
André Cerveira

Escola Superior de Artes e Design, Matosinhos, Portugal
Mafalda Vaz Pinto Moreira

Faculdade de Arquitectura da Universidade Técnica de Lisboa, Lisbon, Portugal
Diana de Sousa Matoso

Elisava Escola Superior de Disseny, Barcelona, Spain
Eduard Riu Domínguez
Mario Escudero Robla

Universidade de Aveiro, Aveiro, Portugal,
Pedro Almeida

Design Academy Eindhoven, the Netherlands
Tina Roeder
Jarrod Beglinger
Kuniko Maeda
Kythzia Barrera Suarez
Lin Chia-Hui

Pratt Institute, New York, U.S.A.
Patrick Best
Dan Hancock
Michelle Zatta
Eric Whiteley
Joseph Hammett

Workshop 'Beyond consumption' by Martí Guixé

Workshop theme:
the Meta-Territorial Kitchen – a Contemporary Kitchen

Introduction: the Moscow Kitchen debate by Nixon and Khrushchev

Charles and Ray Eames were commissioned to design a kitchen for the American National Exhibit in Moscow in 1959. This space technology inspired kitchen, was extremely popular with the Russian public, generating long queues to enter the pavilion and creating far more interest than the space and war technology displayed in the same exhibit, due in part to the cold war.

The kitchen also generated a socio-political debate between Nixon and Khrushchev when they visited the pavilion on July 24th, 1959. This debate is called 'The kitchen debate' and was published the following day in the New York Times.

http://www.cnn.com/SPECIALS/cold.war/episodes/14/documents/debate/

Concept 1: The kitchen as interface
The kitchen is neither a studio, nor a laboratory, but an interface where we work with resources that we can open or not, install, uninstall, execute etc. The basis is an open, operative platform.

Concept 2: Open source code system
Everybody can design new tools that are based in the operative system.

The Meta-Territorial Kitchen is not another re-styling of an existing kitchen but a truly contemporary one. It is an operating system comprising a simple, basic unit that can be improved. Based on the idea of an open source code system, new appliances and tools to prepare food will be developed.

Martí Guixé
31st March 2003

KS-3 open source kitchen system with 6 models made by Martí Guixé

Students in the workshop with Martí Guixé
Patrick Best, Dan Hancock, Tina Roeder, Jarrod Beglinger, Kuniko Maeda, Kythzia Barrera Suarez, Charleen Lin Chia-Hui, Daniel Teles Caramelo, João Sabino

Skills developed with the students:
Systems concept
Idea scouting
Presentation protocols
Professional-casual working
Techniques of self promotion

Developing tools for the KS-3 open source kitchen system

The students worked with colored paper.
Patrick Best: light green
Kythzia Barrera Suarez: cadmium red
Dan Hancock: sky blue
Jarrod Beglinger: yellow
Tina Roeder: brown)
Kuniko Maeda: pink
João Sabino: orange
Daniel Teles Caramelo: white
Charlene Lin Chia-Hui: black
Martí Guixé: dark blue

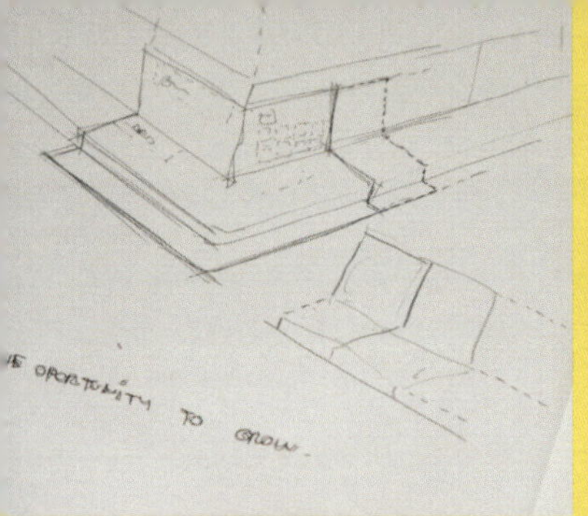
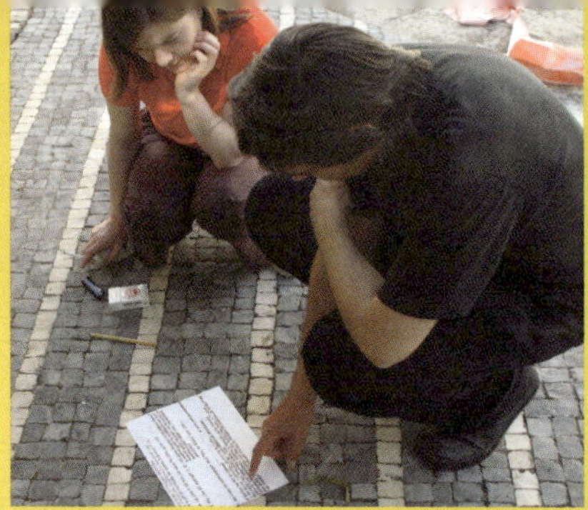
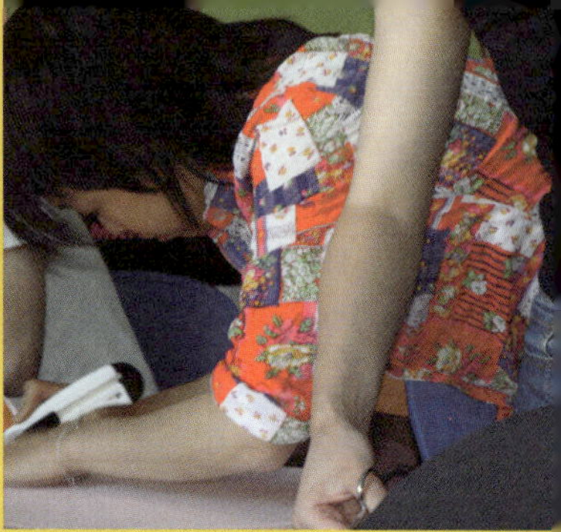
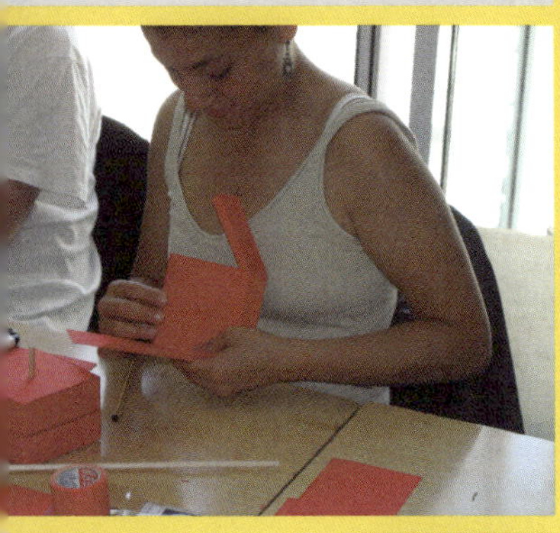
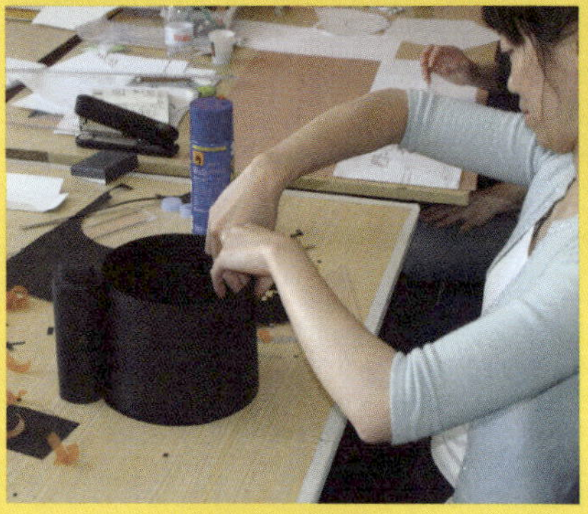
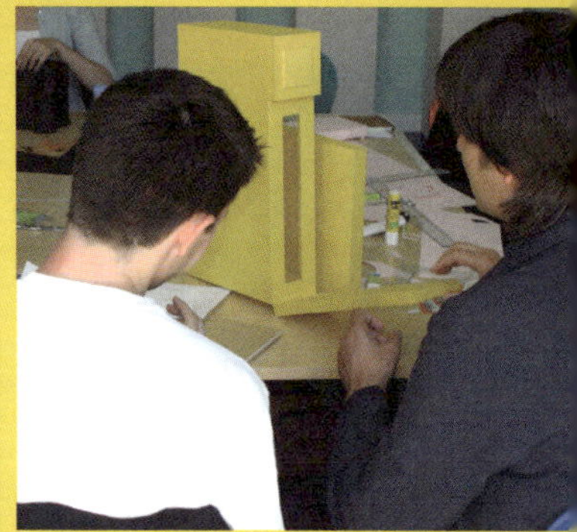
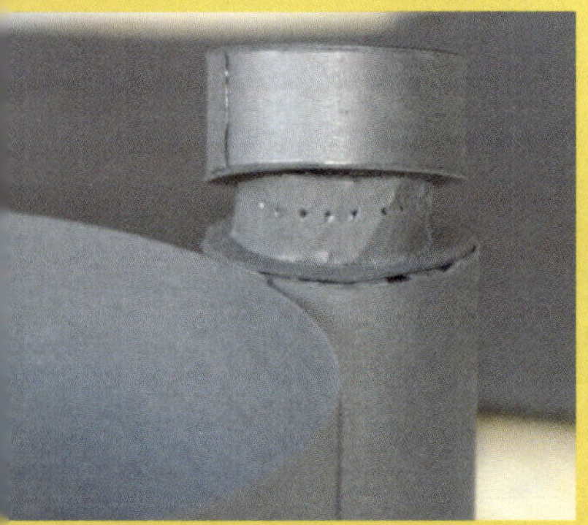
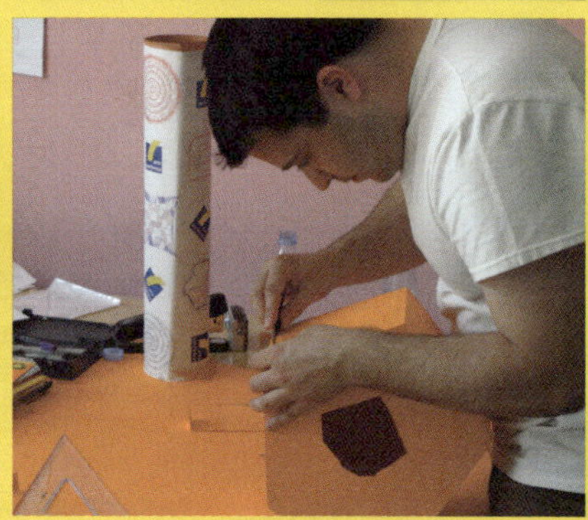
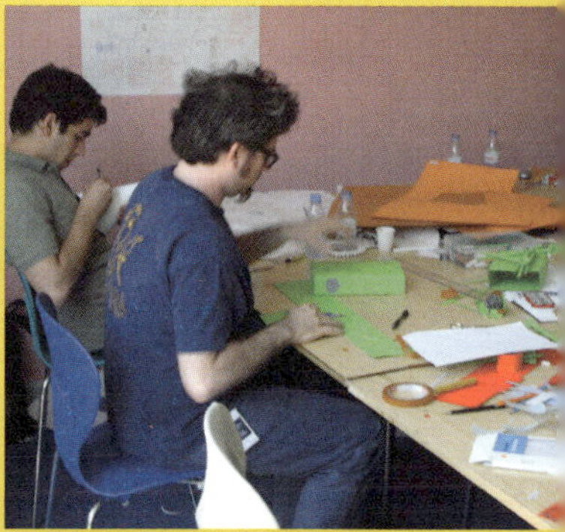
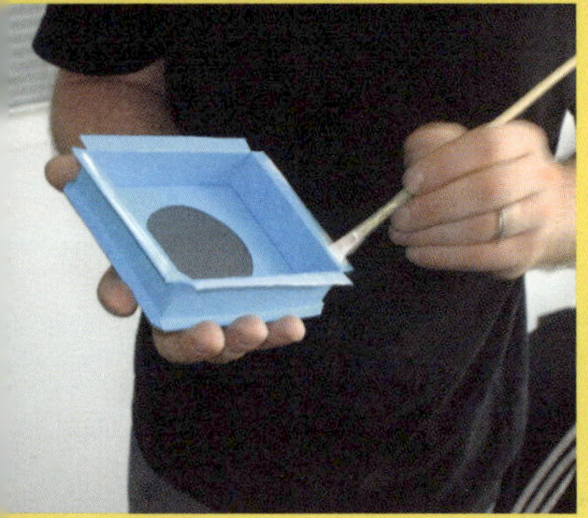
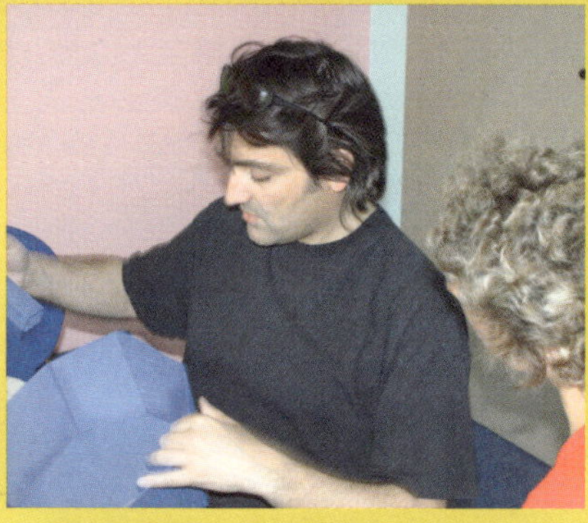
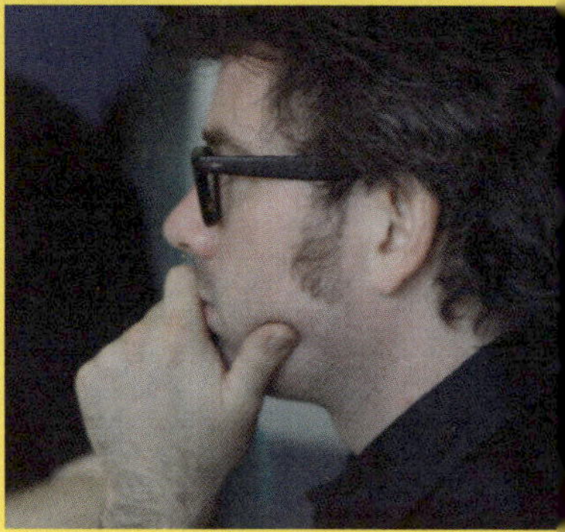
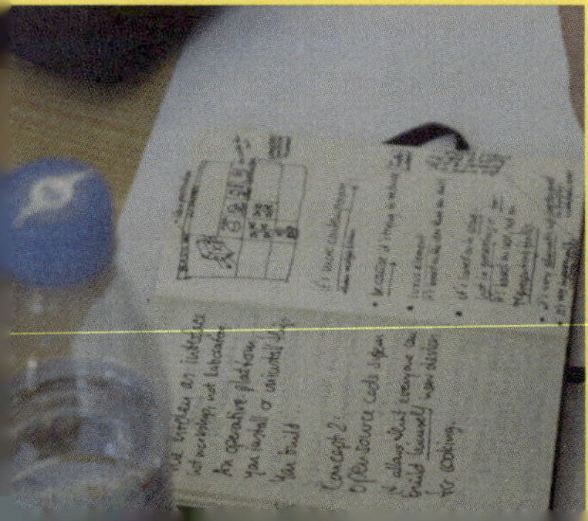
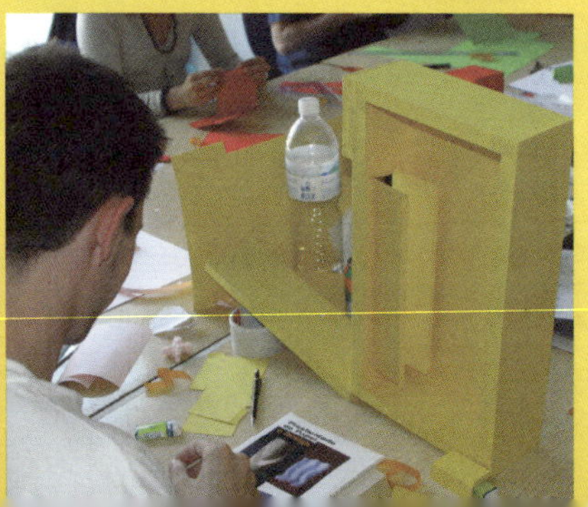
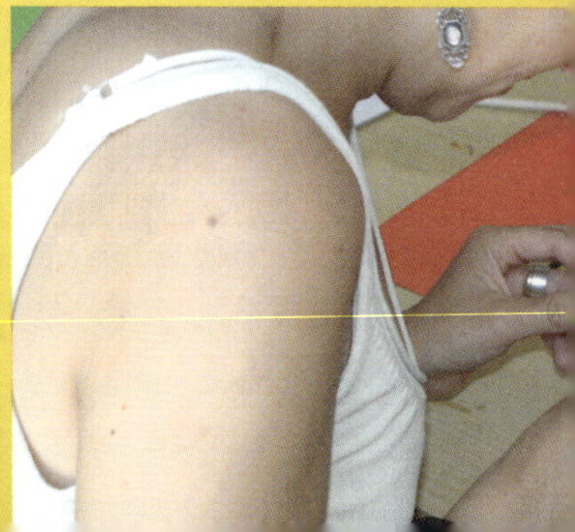

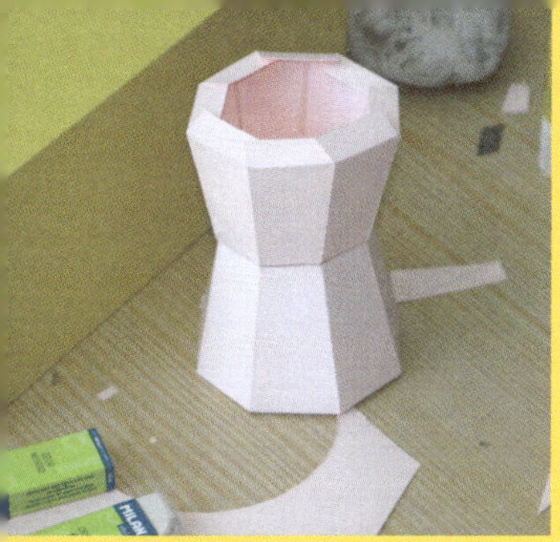

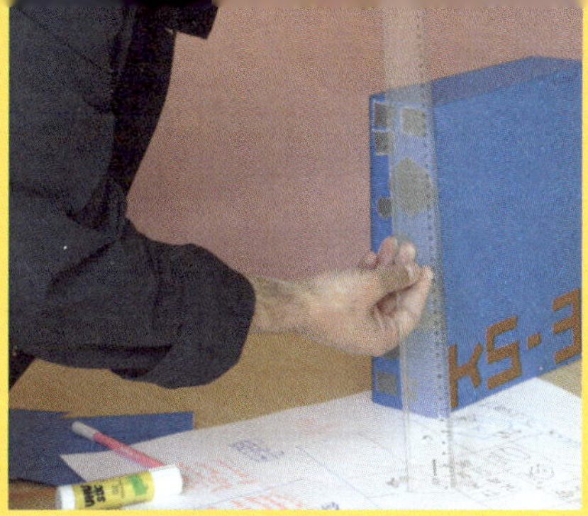
KS-3

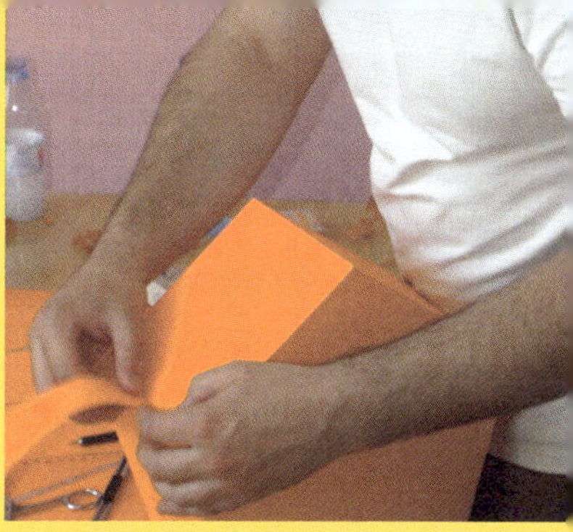

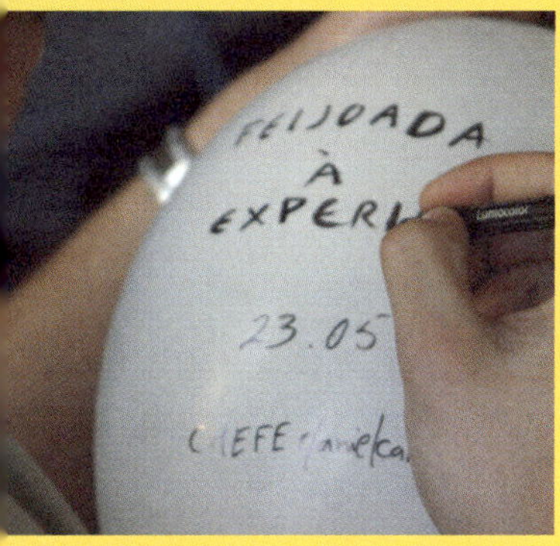
FEIJOADA
À
23.05

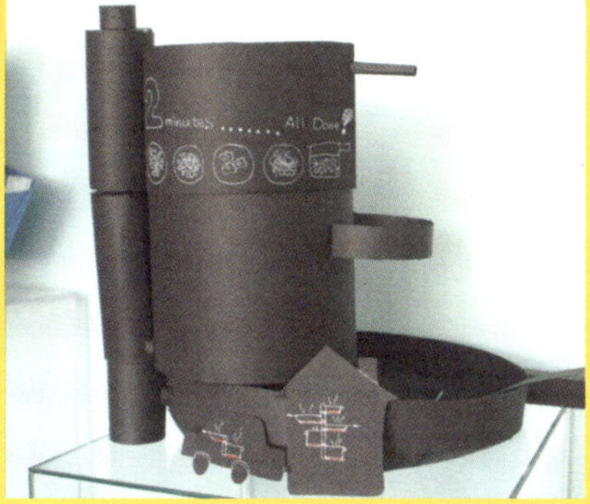

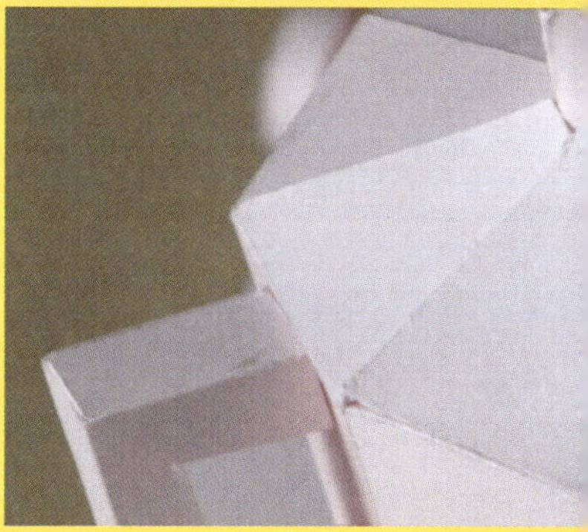

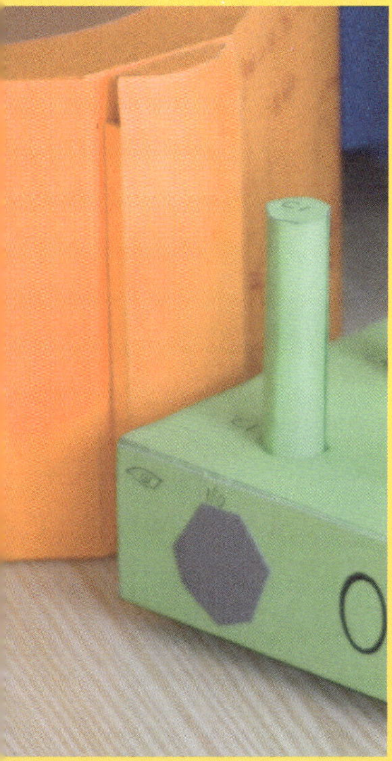

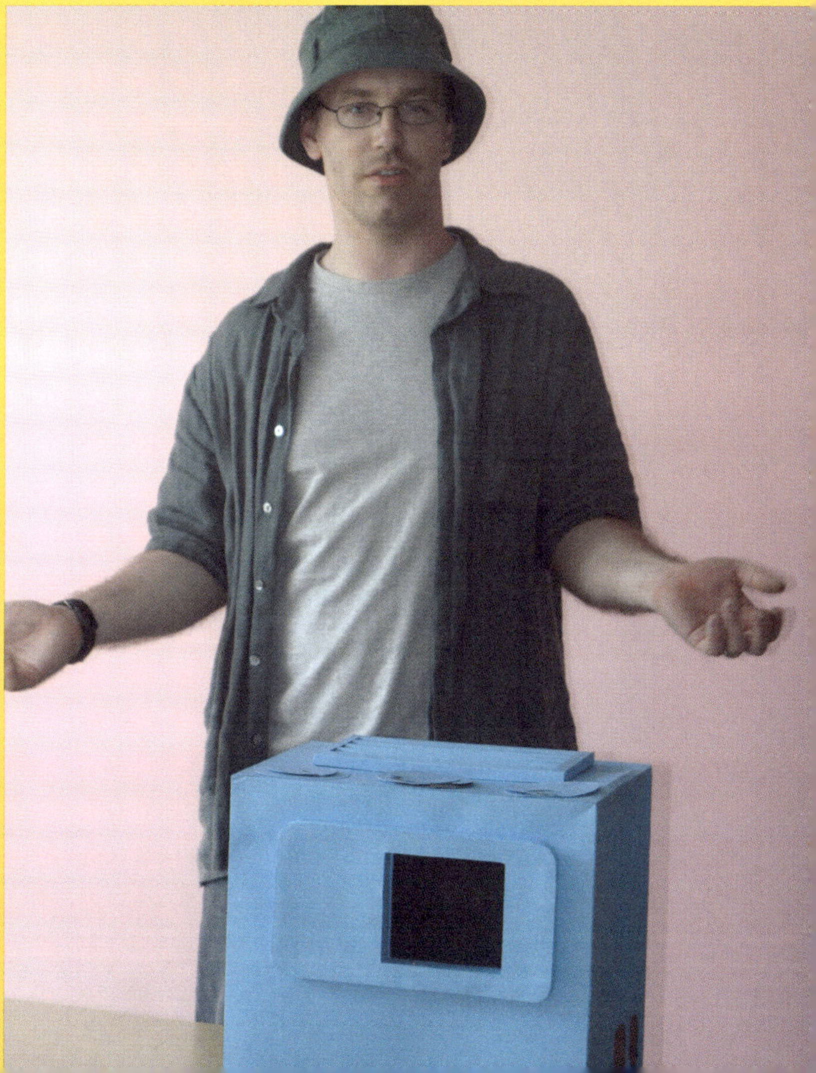

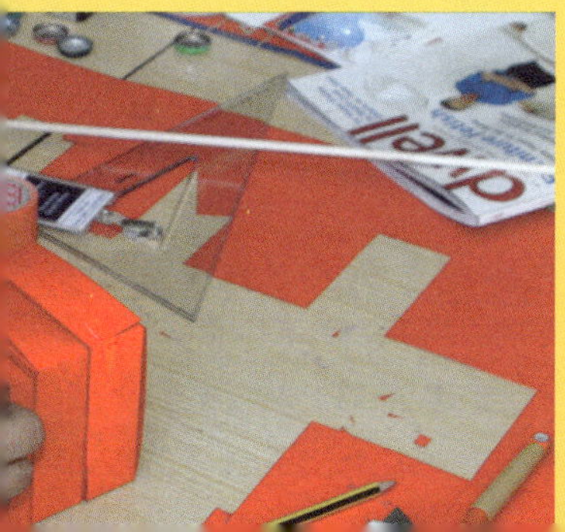

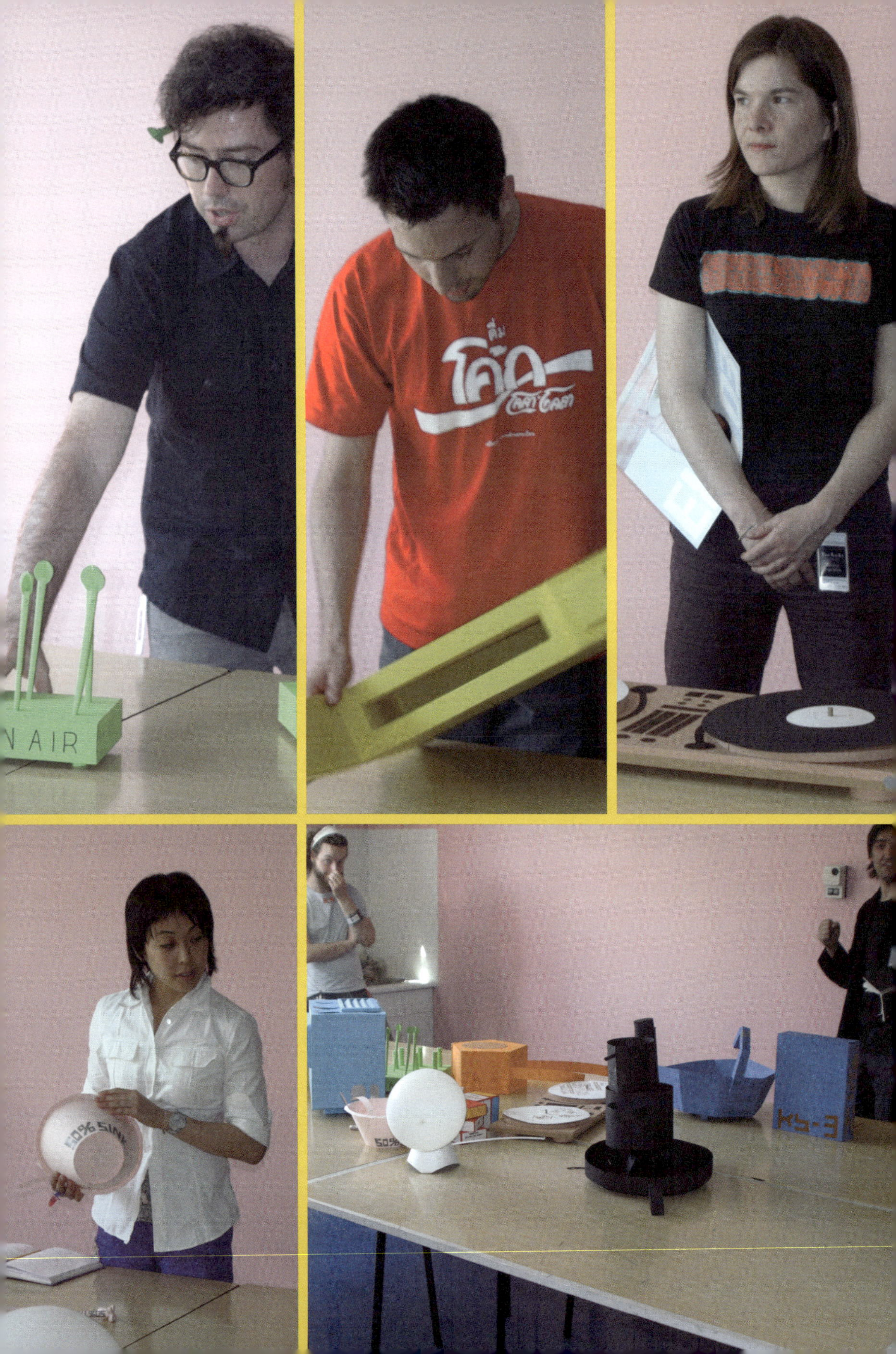
N AIR
50% SINK

Workshop report by Martí Guixé

Daniel: white paper
Smell: filling station
A tool to store odours for any purpose
Martí's comment: the KS-3 allows the creation of elements with no context; anything can be inserted into the kitchen system. At last there is a possibility for new thinking, free from conventions and tradition.

Kitzia: cadmium red paper
Esoteric cube
Martí's comment: the object has a non-physical link to the KS-3. I liked the idea of experimenting with the non-functional element of cooking. The open source makes these kinds of customisations an attitude towards cooking.

Patrick: light green paper
Sound Kitchen studio
Martí's comment: adaptability makes it possible to explore and discover new uses, things can also be transformed temporarily, or for specific occasions. This project has incredible commercial possibilities.

Martí: dark blue paper
KS-3 the system
Martí's comment: a platform for cooking that permits the user to connect, disconnect, configure, change move and transport depending on time and use.

Charlene: black paper
Multi-tasking cooking
Martí's comment: a stove for multiple cooking, it explores other ways of cooking without making permanent irreversible decisions, it enables sharing important cooking tools or giving them as presents.

João: orange paper
Picnic unit
Martí's comment: the system allows connectivity without losing the same capacities as at home. It represents the idea of cooking in extreme situations.

Dan: sky blue paper
Window maker
Martí's comment: this represents the idea of common kitchen design components (like a window). By emulating them the traditional objects disappear, but not the function. It is a kind of displacement of the conventional context.

Kuniko: pink paper
50% more multi-functional
Martí's comment: by reducing the dimension of the cooking appliances by 50% without reducing the functions, the tools acquire an entirely new range of possibilities. For example, an extreme situation like one-pot cooking.

Jarrod: yellow paper
Computer dinner
Martí's comment: this permits the KS-3 to give you the option of changing your diet by easily changing your kitchen, without the problems associated with building and rebuilding fixed situations. Allows for changing life-styles

Tina: brown paper
DJ kitchen station
Martí's comment: It is about the de-contextualization of activities through the de-contextualization of the room and lifestyle. It means that time spent waiting can be filled and facilitates social interchange in the cooking area.

Workshop 'Beyond consumption' by Jurgen Bey

Introduction:
Learning from India: rubbish and dust

Travelling through India gave me a new understanding of rubbish and its functions. Small things became big, strange associations were made and the richness of rubbish became apparent.

In India there is so much dust everywhere. Questions like 'what is the function of dust?' kept running through my mind. It will slowly turn the world grey and reduce everything to the same level. Just imagine no difference between who is who and what is what – a wastebasket or a cash-box look the same.

Then things will be used for what they are really good at. If you can totally close yourself so that nobody can enter, you will become a cash-box. And if you are totally open, so that everybody can put things in, you will become a wastebasket.

Being both dusty and grey, trading places will be a real possibility. The cash-box can become a wastebasket and the wastebasket can become a cash-box. Everyone can fill the wastebasket-cash-box and if you think you need it, you can take out whatever you need. If the cash-box becomes a wastebasket, all the rubbish it has gathered can never get out. Then slowly all waste will be absorbed and the world will become clean forever.

Or imagine that dust and waste become valuable. India would be the wealthiest country on earth. Finally having nothing becomes the greatest wealth you can achieve.

Just look at the quality of things.

Theme: How rubbish and people can come together and form a new order.
Learning from India, we are going to build a New World in five days.
This week we will not say that rubbish shouldn't be here. Rubbish is everywhere. We will look in the streets for rubbish and try to find its good qualities and how it can be transformed into something new and useful. We will start with a completely empty mind, without a preconceived plan or direction.

We need:
– Rubbish: things from the house that are no longer wanted or needed or just need to be replaced
– Pictures or images collected from home, things that have lost their personal value
– 100 questions about rubbish and its future.
– Newspaper or other thin white paper that can be used to make papier-mâché, our material to form and pack things
– Wallpaper glue to make the papier-mâché
– White latex paint to paint the resulting objects white
– Household plastic to wrap things in
– A camera to document the process

Jurgen Bey
April 2003

FRAGIL
FRAGIL
WE TAPE
EVERYTHIN
MANY THINGS
WE FIND
WE THINK
WE WANT

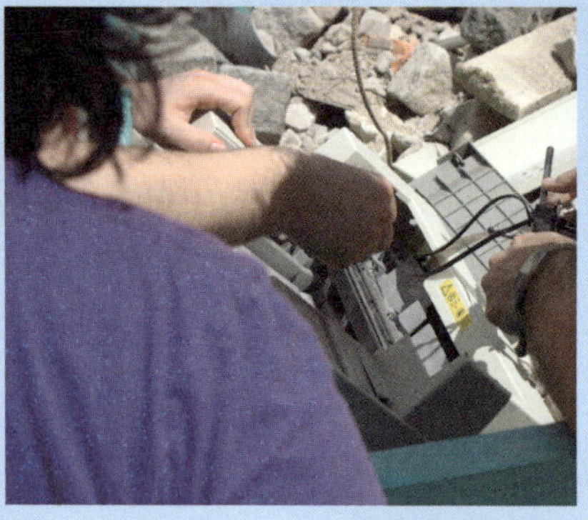

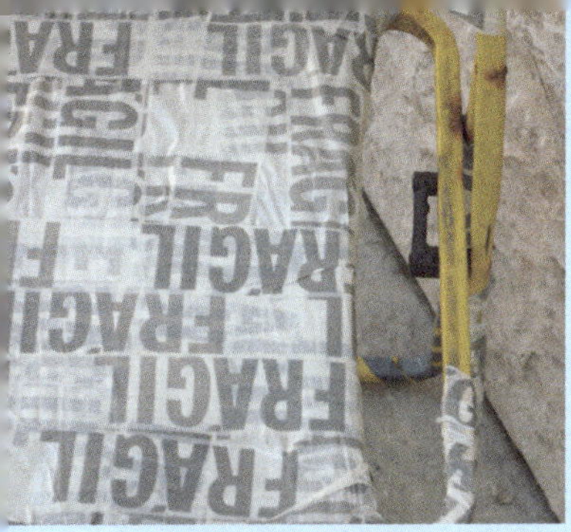
FRAGIL

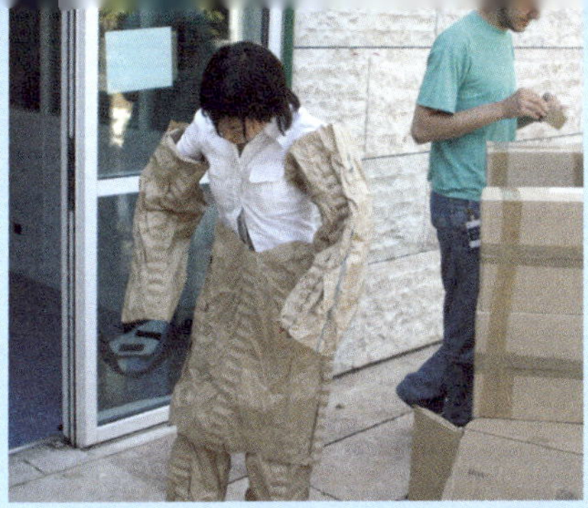

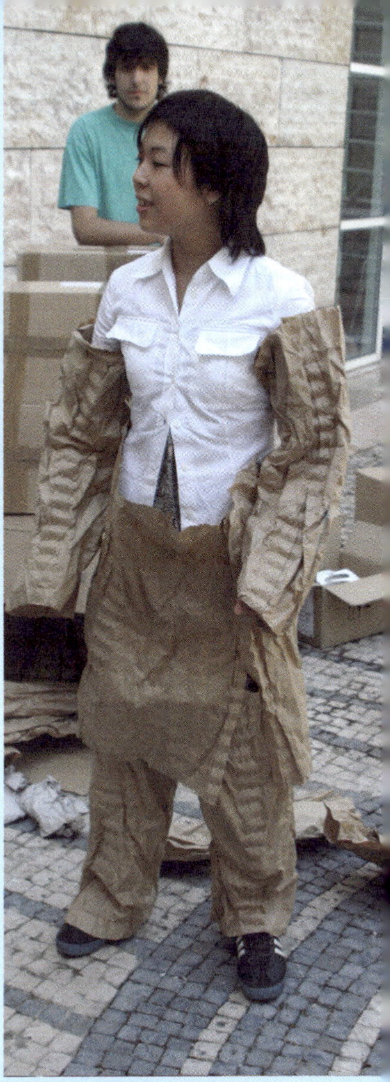

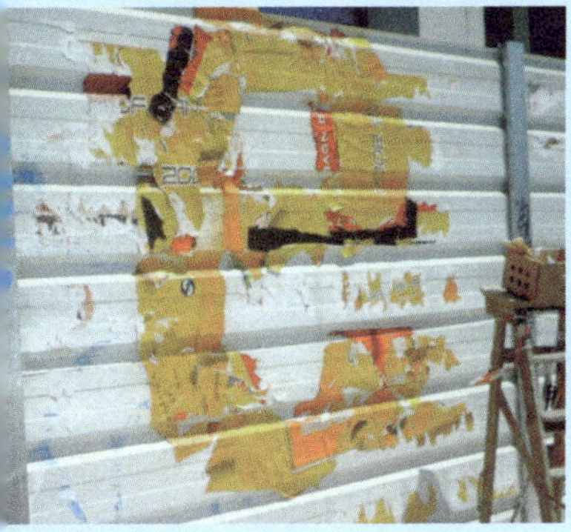

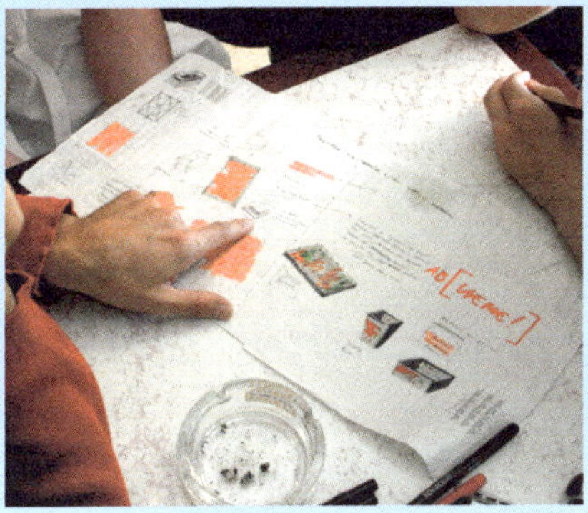

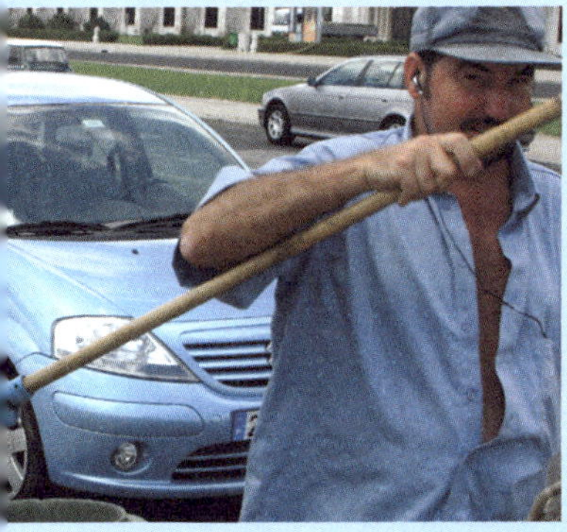

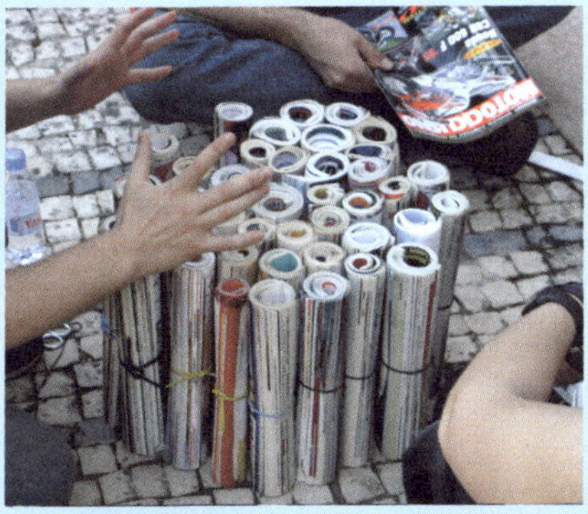

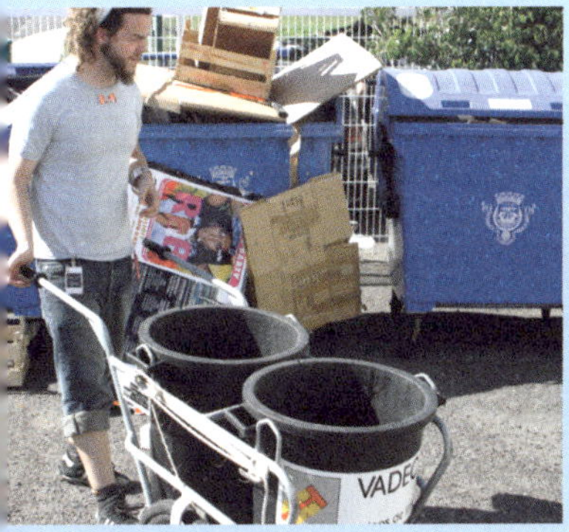

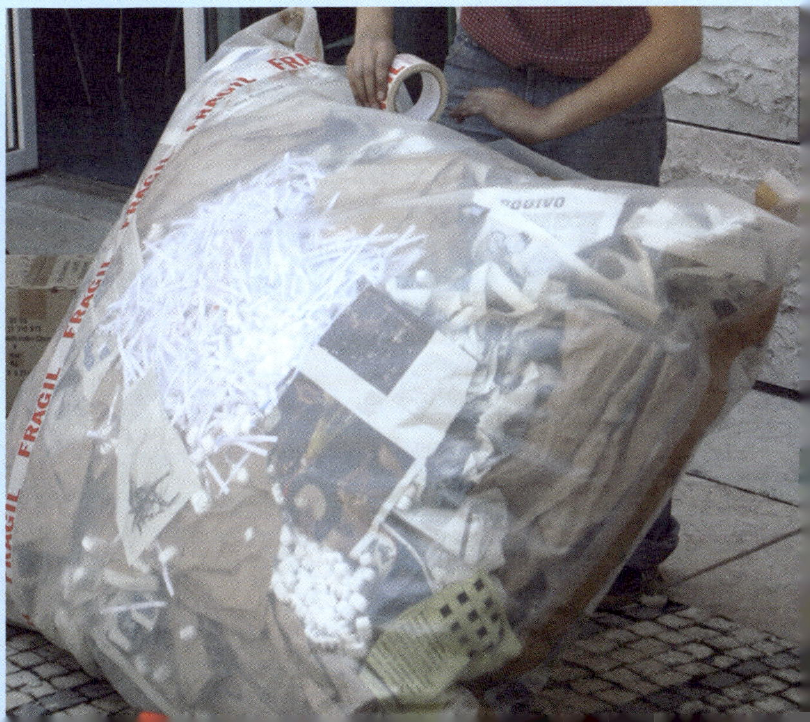
FRAGIL

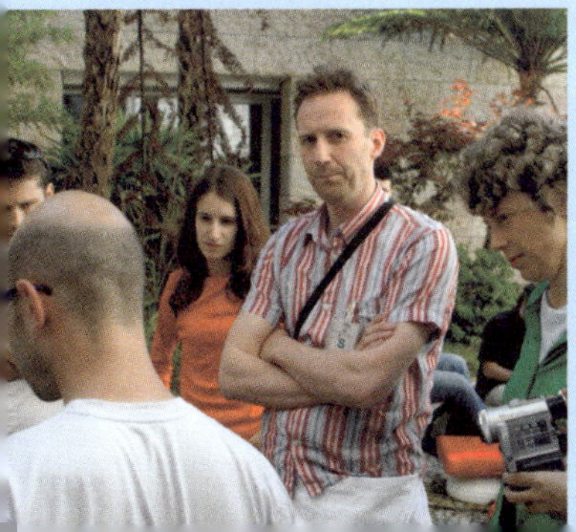

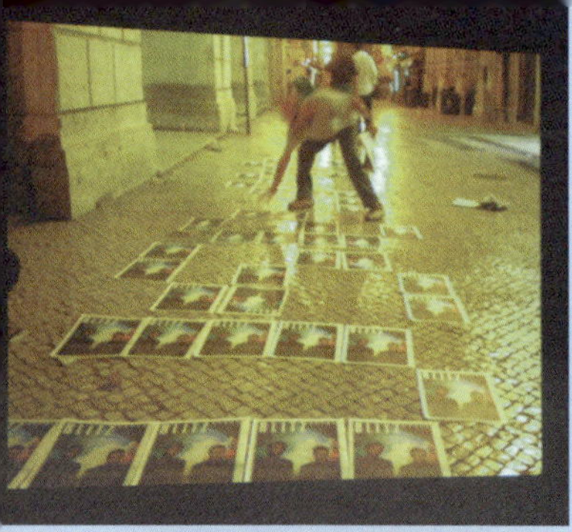

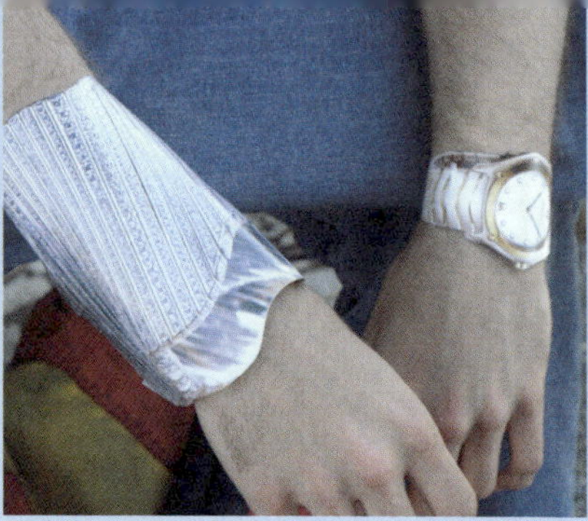

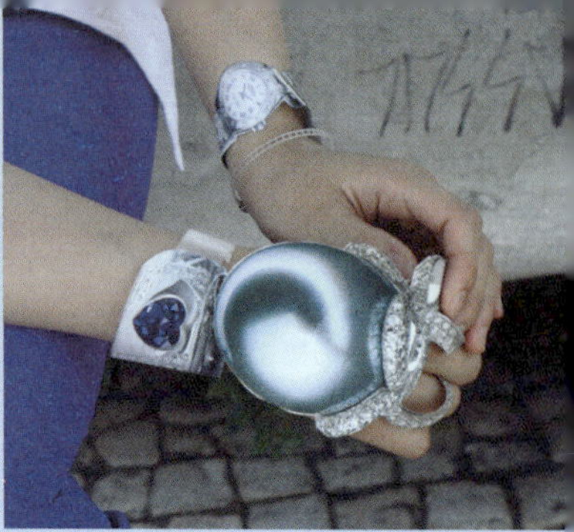

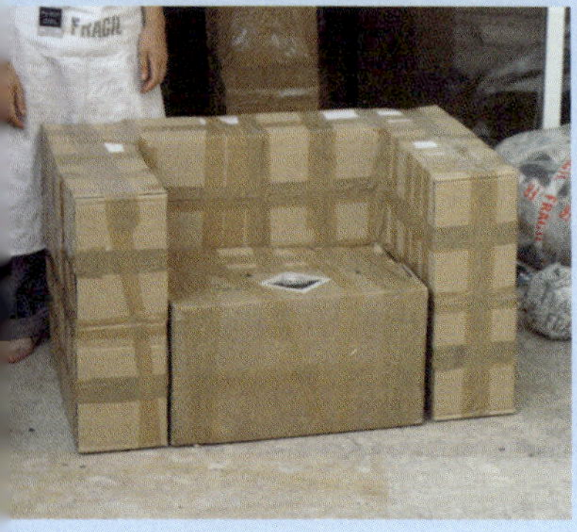

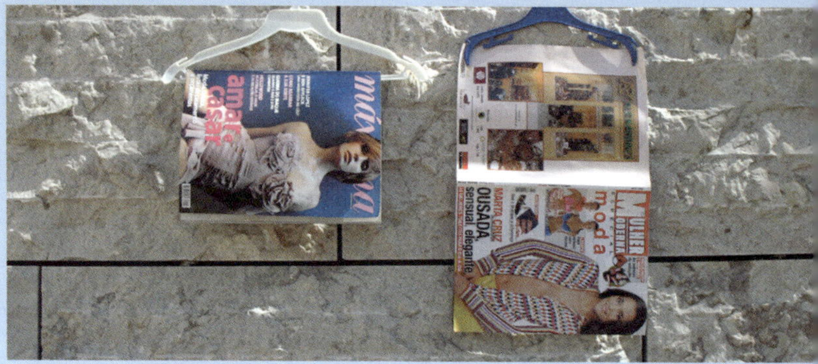

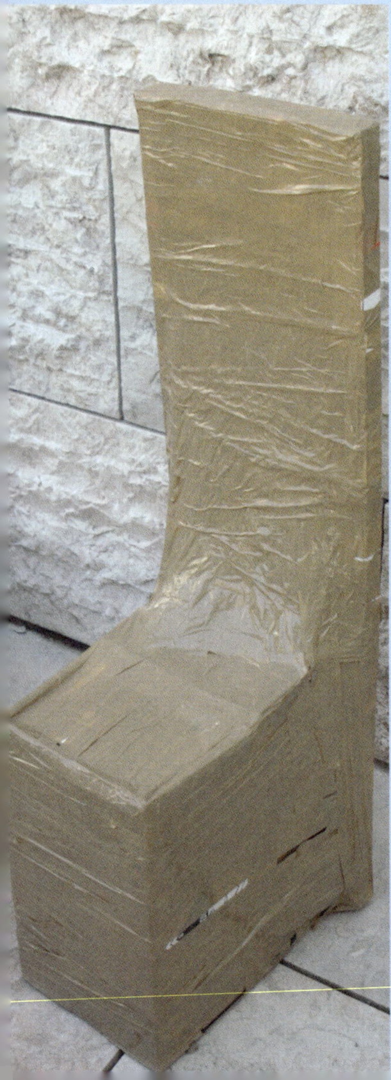

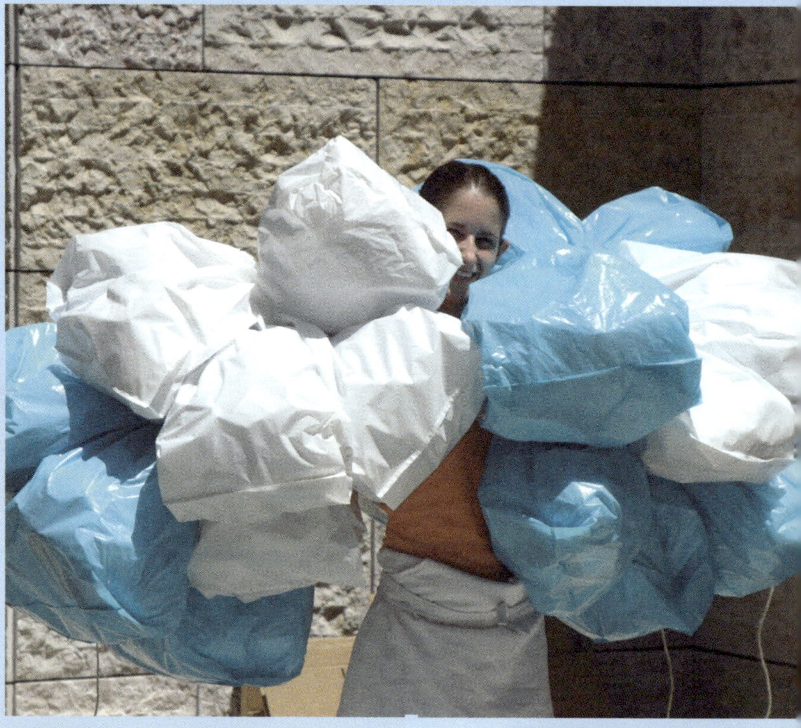

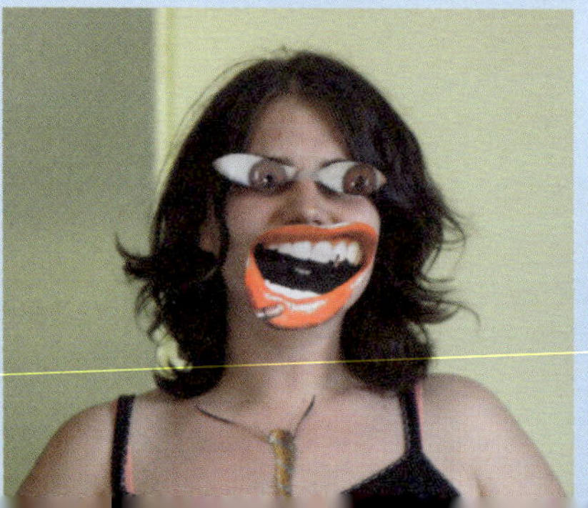

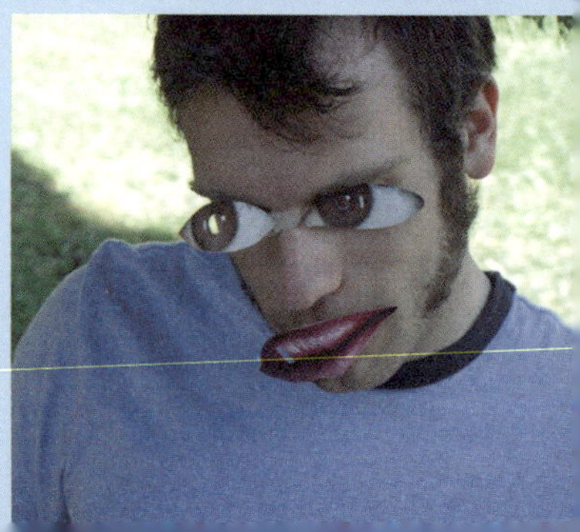

Workshop report by Jurgen Bey

December 2001
In 2001 I made a study trip to India. This is now more than a year ago, during which time the questions have continued to sing around my head. Through lectures they are constantly tossed in the air and until now have not landed. India offered many new insights but answered none of the questions. The world turned upside-down; I returned with more questions than when I left; apparently looking cannot provide the answers.

December 2002
The Linen-chest-house project is a quest for a new order for junk; things that no longer work or are no longer wanted always retain their meaning, by arranging them anew, close to the world they already know, they give a new perspective to the ordinary. Box bed, four-poster bed, hut-building, sleeping under the stars. Actually the useless linen chest in the attic wanted to become a wendy-house. Together with beautiful, almost forgotten blankets and an old table they form the linen-chest-house. No street value; a bedecked four-poster bed in the garden.

The Linen-chest-house project, (2002, see page 182-183) was designed as the initial response to my trip to India.

April 2003
Students were flown in from all over the world to participate in a workshop about the world of consumerism and to consider what we had to say about it.

See Buy Fly
As with the wendy-house, we began by assembling existing things and attempting to re-arrange them until a new order was reached, which did not get us much further but which certainly offered new possibilities.

Without a preconceived order or idea we began to collect worthless junk. All of it supposedly necessary to create and sell a new world. After three days of rummaging, without direction and without knowing what the others were doing, an ordered over-all concept slowly emerged.

The four logos count as the workshop's conclusion.

1-Advertising-billboard-space
In order to ensure that we know what we need and where we can get it there exists an enormous infrastructure of billboards, which can define the face of the city.

Disorganised fly-posters that attract attention through their graphic design and their quantity. A temporary phenomenon that creates beauty and cleans through renewal. The use-by date is part of the system. Everything that we paste over disappears and is absorbed in space. Slowly entire houses and office-blocks come into being, which constantly reinvent themselves. Advertising billboard space for nothing that can absorb disorder. Use me!

Lifestyle-Magazine-Makeup
The world of magazines has become our oracle. Glossy paper tells us what to do, what to wear, where to buy and where to be. The products represent a lifestyle but retain a body that we must bear. If the magazine becomes the product, why should the products require three-dimensional form? Everything is and remains paper, the world as make-up. The products are allowed to come out of the magazine to be worn, only to reappear as reportage in the next glossy mag. Eventually the products redevelop themselves with the frequency of the lifestyle magazines. Ravishing pictures through which to live. Piles of magazines like Pandora's box.

Sale-discount-label
To sell we must renew, to ensure that we have room for the new we must sell, we must sell-out. High-cost stickers and labels developed for the sales to mark down products to low value. Everything we leave behind disappears in the stickers

and paper. Keep sticking until the world values them once again. The paper label.

Shopping-bag-day
Because we want to have so much we continue to buy. To carry our purchases we have plastic bags, which show where we bought them. They have become mobile messengers. Mountains of products that end up in, on and around the wardrobe. Maybe we can introduce a shopping-bag-day, the day of the great clear-out. A festival in which we get rid of the things we no longer want. Bags grow into costumes and parade like floats through the streets. Valueless products drive us, organised to order things anew.

September 2003
Like a disorderly relay race I seek the value of so-called junk. The future is to be continued.

Jurgen Bey
August 2003

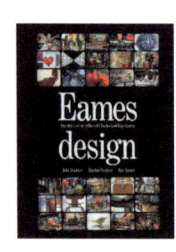

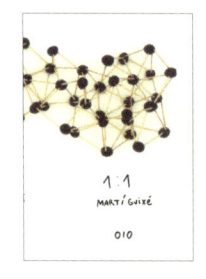

Literature

Many books have been published about design in the last 50 years. Some of them have the intention to bring us new values, new ideas and considerations about the world and it sources. We made a selection of books that question the design culture and design economics with many different local or global perspectives. All of these books are magnificent sources to pick up bright ideas that can change our attitude towards industrial and economic production.

Volker Albus, *'Wohnen von Sinnen'*, 1986
VolkerAlbus/Michel Feith/Rouli Lecatsa/
Wolfgang Schepers/Claudia Schneider-Esleben, Frankfurt
ISBN 3770119282

Emilio Ambasz, *'The New Domestic Landscape,'*
1972. Publisher: Museum Of Modern Art,
New York

Rolf-Peter Baacke, Uta Brandes and Michael Erlhoff, *'Design als Gegenstand'*, 1984
Frölich&Kaufmann, Berlin
ISBN 3887250982

Conny Bakker and Ed Van Hinte, *'Trespassers – inspiration for eco-efficient design'*, 1998
010 Publishers, Rotterdam
ISBN 9064503753

Andrea Branzi, *'The Hot House: Italian new wave design'*, 1984
Thames & Hudson, London
ISBN 0500273480

Lucius Burckhardt, Hans Höger, *'Design ist unsichtbar'*, 1995
Hatje Cantz Verlag, Hans Höger
ISBN 3893227652

Lucius Burckhardt, *'Die Kinder fressen ihre Revolution'*, 1995
Du Mont Reiseverlag, Koln
ISBN 3770117182

Eames Demetrios, *'An Eames Primer'*, 2001
Universe Publishing, New York
ISBN 0789306298

Jean Clair, *'Des Européens'*, 1997
Maison Européenne de la Photographie/Seuil
ISBN 2904732810

Gillo Dorfles, *'Il Disegno Industriale e la sua Estetica'* or *'Gute Industrieform und ihre Ästhetik'*, 1963
Capelli Editore, Bologna and Verlag Moderne Industrie, Munich

Beppe Finessi, *'Bruno Munari'*, 1999
Cosmit Fair Organisation, Milan

Mieke Gerritzen *'Everyone is a designer'*, 1998
BIS Publishers, Amsterdam
ISBN 9072007697

Martí Guixé, *'Libre de contexte'*, 2003
Birkhäuser Verlag
ISBN 3764324228

Ed van Hinte, *'Martí Guixé, 1:1'*, 2002
Introduction by Paola Antonelli and Octavi Rofes
010 Publishers, Rotterdam
ISBN 8492110325

Ed Van Hinte, *'Eternally yours – visions on product design'*, 1997
010 Publishers, Rotterdam
ISBN 9064503133

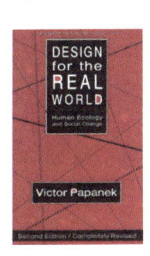

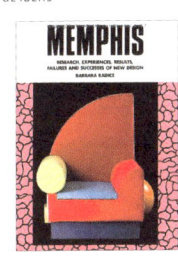

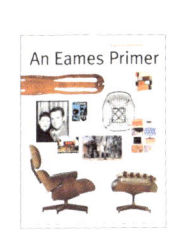

Lichtenstein and Häberli, *'Air Made Visible. A visual reader on Bruno Munari'*, 2000
Lars Müller Publishers
ISBN 3907044894

Bruno Munari, *'Design as art,'* Penguin Books, Harmonds Worth, 1971
ISBN 0140212663

John Neuhart, Marilyn Neuhart and Ray Eames, *'Eames Design'*, 1989
Harry N. Abrams, New York
ISBN 0810908794

Victor Papanek, *'Design for the real world'*, 1979
Thames & Hudson, London
ISBN 0500273588
Academy Chicago Pub; 2nd Revision edition (February 1999)
ISBN 0897331532

Barbara Radice, *'Memphis: research, experience, failures and successes of new design'*, 1995 (reprint)
Thames & Hudson, London
ISBN 0500273774

Renny Ramakers, *'Droog Design in context'*, 2002
010 Publishers, Rotterdam
ISBN 9064504571

Aldo Tanchis, Bruno Munari, *'Design as Art'*, Penguin Books, U.S.A.
ISBN 0140212663

John Thackara, *'Design after Modernism'*, 1987
Thames & Hudson, London
ISBN 0500234833

Liesbeth Waechter-Böhm, *'Design ist unsichtbar'*, 1980/81.
Österreichisches Institut für Visuelle Gestaltung
ISBN 385409020

Bruce Bernard, *'Century'*, 2001
Phaidon, London
ISBN 0714838489

David Frankel, *'Walker Evans & Company'*, 2000
The Museum of Modern Art, New York
ISBN 0870700324

'America in Passing', U.S.A. 1935-1975
Photographs by Henri Cartier-Bresson
Introduction by Gilles Mora
Henri Cartier-Bresson and Editions de Sieul Paris, 1991,
ISBN 0500541698

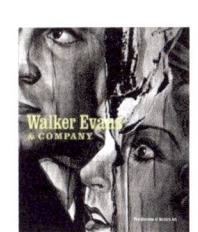

'Bright Minds, Beautiful Ideas'

The workshop, the exhibition and this book are initiated by Ed Annink
on the occasion of **ExperimentaDesign 2003 - Bienal de Lisboa**, Lisbon, Portugal.

Centro de Exposições, Centro Cultural de Belém – Museu do Design, Lisbon, Portugal.
September 18 to November 30, 2003,

Kunsthal Rotterdam, the Netherlands.
Spring 2004

EXHIBITION

Co-production:
ExperimentaDesign 2003 – Bienal de Lisboa, Lisbon, Portugal
Centro Cultural de Belém – Museu do Design, Lisbon, Portugal
Kunsthal, Rotterdam, the Netherlands

Text: Ed Annink, Jurgen Bey, Martí Guixé, Ineke Schwartz
Design: Ontwerpwerk, *office for design*, Jons Jeronimus and Ed Annink, The Hague, the Netherlands
Constructions: Cenycet, Lisbon, Portugal
Translations: *Dutch-English:* Gerard Forde, Holden Translations
English-Portuguese: Graça Margarido

Financial supported by
Mondriaan Foundation, Amsterdam, the Netherlands

Powered by Canon
LV-S2 Beamers, EOS 10D Camera's, Panels printed on Canons BJ-W9000, W7200/W7250, W8200D/W8200P using Canon Ink & Media: Large format printing at the highest quality. Prints are laminated with Canon's TS-4400

Supported by
Eames Office, Santa Monica, U.S.A.
Ontwerpwerk, *office for design*, The Hague, the Netherlands

BOOK

Publisher: BIS Publishers, Amsterdam
Edited by Ed Annink and Ineke Schwartz
Text: Ed Annink, Jurgen Bey, Martí Guixé, Timo de Rijk, Louise Schouwenberg, Ineke Schwartz
Translations: *Dutch-English:* Gerard Forde, Lynn George, Holden Translations, Wendie Shaffer
Design: Ontwerpwerk, *office for design*, Stephan Csikós, The Hague, the Netherlands
Printing: Drukkerij Slinger BV, Alkmaar, the Netherlands
Print run: 3500 copies

Financial supported by
Banco BPI, Portugal
ExperimentaDesign 2003 – Bienal de Lisboa, Lisbon, Portugal
Foundation Products of Imagination, the Netherlands

Supported by
Vitra Design Museum, Weil am Rhein, Germany
Eames Office, Santa Monica, U.S.A.
Ontwerpwerk, *office for design*, The Hague, the Netherlands

Acknowledgements
Guta Moura Guedes, João Paulo Feliciano, Pedro Gadanho, Martí Guixé, Jurgen Bey, Alfredo Häberli, Rolf Fehlbaum, Alexander von Vegesack, Eames Demetrios, Jonas Mekas, Wim Pijbes, Bruno Sequeira, Rita Morgado, Jeroen van Pelt, Renny Ramakers, Max Bruinsma, Ed van Hinte, Rudolf van Wezel, Mana Yildiz, Yael Kovalivker, Elisabetta Jezek, Wouter Peltenburg, Jeroen Thomas, Yvonne le Grand.

B/SPUBLISHERS

WORKSHOP

Centro de Exposições Centro Cultural de Belém – Museu do Design, Lisbon, Portugal
May 19th to May 23rd, 2003

Students in the workshop with Martí Guixé

Patrick Best, Dan Hancock, Tina Roeder, Jarrod Beglinger, Kuniko Maeda, Kythzia Barrera Suarez, Charleen Lin Chia-Hui, Daniel Teles Caramelo, João Sabino.

Students in the workshop with Jurgen Bey

Michelle Zatta, Eric Whiteley, André Cerveira, Joseph Hammett, Mafalda Vaz Pinto Moreira, Diana de Sousa Matoso, Eduard Riu Domínguez, Mario Escudero Robla, Pedro Almeida.

Participating schools

Faculdade de Belas Artes de Lisboa, Lisbon, Portugal
Escola Superior de Tecnologia, Gestão, Arte e Design, Caldas da Rainha, Portugal
Instituto de Artes Visuais, Design e Marketing, Lisbon, Portugal
Escola Superior de Artes e Design, Matosinhos, Portugal
Faculdade de Arquitectura da Universidade Técnica de Lisboa, Lisbon, Portugal
Elisava Escola Superior de Disseny, Barcelona, Spain
Universidade de Aveiro, Aveiro, Portugal
Design Academy Eindhoven, the Netherlands
Pratt Institute, New York, U.S.A.

Internet links

www.dolcevita.com/design/designers/munar
www.eamesoffice.com
www.guixe.com
www.jurgenbey.nl

www.experimentadesign.pt
www.brightmindsbeautifulideas.org

www.canon.com
www.ontwerpwerk.com
www.productsofimagination.nl
www.vitra-museum.de

www.inekeschwartz.nl
www.timoderijk.nl
www.edannink.com

EXPERIMENTADESIGN2003
BIENAL DE LISBOA / 17 SET / 02 NOV

Ontwerpwerk
office for design

poi [products of imagination]®

BPI

you can
Canon

Photocredits

Photos from Vitra Design Museum Archive.
Page: 62, 63, 70, 74, 75. Scans from the original 'House of Cards' and 'Giant House of Cards' which we had as a loan from Vitra Design Museum. Page: 67, 73

Scans of images from *'An Eames Primer.'* Page: 54, 69, 64
©2003 Lucia Eames dba Eames Office (www.eamesoffice.com)

Scans of images from *'Eames Design, The work of the Office of Charles and Ray Eames.'* Page: 60, 71

Images from *'Bruno Munari, Air Made Visible'*
Page: 37, 39, 41, 42, 43, 44, 45, 46, 47

Image from *'Bruno Munari'.* Page: 48

Image from *'Le Machine di Munari'.* Page: 39

Scan (with retouche) is made of the cover from the catalogue *'Bruno Munari.'* Page: 28

Photo's by Martí Guixé. Page: 150, 151, 152, 153, 154, 155, 156, 157, 158, 159, 160, 161, 162, 163, 164, 165

Illustrations by Martí Guixé. Page: 9, 118, 125, 126, 127, 128, 129, 140, 141, 142, 143, 144, 145, 146, 147

Photos by Inga Knoelke (Image Kontainer). Page: 108, 109, 110, 111, 112, 113, 114, 115, 116, 117, 121, 122, 123, 130

Photo's by Jurgen Bey. Page: 208, 209, 210, 211, 212, 213, 214, 215, 216, 217, 186, 187, 189

Images on the illustration pages of Jurgen Bey are partly made with images from unknown photographers. Page: 180, 188, 192, 193, 194, 195, 196, 197, 198, 199, 200, 201, 202, 203, 204

Photo's by Bob Goedewagen. Page: 181, 182, 183, 184, 185, 190

Photo's by Jeroen van Pelt. Page: 24, 25, 100, 222, 224, 225, 226, 227, 228, 230, 231, 232

Photo's by Ed Annink. Page: 9, 36, 66, 68, 72, 119, 120, 172, 240
The images of the 'Cacao dune', 'Gin-Tonic puddle' and 'Penellessa' are taken from remakes (made by Ed Annink) for the purpose of this book and the exhibition only.

Photo from unknown photographer. Page: 132

From left to right: Ed Annink, Ineke Schwartz, Timo de Rijk

Some texts and images in the exhibition and book are inspired by, and partly taken from the following books:
'Bruno Munari, Air made visible' by Lichtenstein and Häberli (Lars Müller Publishers) / *'Bruno Munari'* by Beppe Finessi, (Cosmit Fair Organisation, Milan) / *'Le Machine di Munari'* by Bruno Munari (Corraini Publishers, Mantova) / *'Eames Design'* by John Neuhart, Marilyn Neuhart and Ray Eames (Harry N. Abrahams, Inc. Publishers, New York) / *'An Eames Primer'* by Eames Demetrios (Universe Publishing, New York) / *'Martí Guixé, Libre de contexte, context-free/Kontext-frei'* by Chantal Prud'Hom and Martí Guixé, (Mu.dac, Lausanne and Birkhauser, publishers for architecture, Basel-Boston-Berlin) / *'Martí Guixé, 1:1'* by Ed van Hinte, (010 Publishers, Rotterdam) / *'Organic Design'* catalogue, MoMA New York, 1941